Debate and Dialogue in Correctional Settings

Debate and Dialogue in Correctional Settings

MAPS, MODELS, AND MATERIALS

Johannes Wheeldon, Ricardo B. Chavez, and Joe Cooke

International Debate Education Association

New York, London & Amsterdam

Published by:

International Debate Education Association
105 East 22nd Street
New York, NY 10010

This book is based on a handbook prepared for Loretta Taylor, Director, Education Programming, Coyote Ridge Corrections Center (CRCC) and Joe Small, Dean of Correctional Education, Walla Walla Community College (WWCC). This book was developed in conjunction with programs at the Coyote Ridge Corrections Center (CRCC), the Washington State Penitentiary (WSP) and the Department of Corrections, Olympia, WA. The authors would like to acknowledge suggestions made by staff at CRCC and the important contributions of students at CRCC, WSP and the CRCC Debate Club.

Debate and Dialogue in Correctional Settings was completed with the generous support from the Youth Initiative, Open Society Foundations, New York, NY.

Library of Congress Cataloging-in-Publication Data

Wheeldon, Johannes.

Debate and dialogue in correctional settings : maps, models, and materials / Johannes Wheeldon, Washington State University; Ricardo B. Chavez, Walla Walla Community College; Joe Cooke, Walla Walla Community College.

pages cm

ISBN 978-1-61770-070-5

1. Debates and debating—Study and teaching. 2. Prisoners—Education—Washington (State). 3. Corrections—Washington (State) I. Chavez, Ricardo B., author. II. Cooke, Joe, author. III. Title.

PN4181.W433 2013

808.53071'5—dc23

2012045947

Design Composition by Kathleen Hayes

Printed in the USA

❦ IDEBATE Press

CONTENTS

FOREWORD

Democracy is not a spectator sport. It requires participation, critical analysis, and engagement with ideas. Yet, in virtually every U.S. state, every Canadian province, and every school district in most countries around the globe, lessons on democratic thought and civic action have been put on the back burner or eliminated altogether. Education goals, broadly speaking, have become increasingly technocratic, individualistic, and narrowly focused on job training. Where lessons in democratic engagement are given, they tend to be opportunistic rather than systematic—based on an individual teacher's courage rather than on programmatic muscle—and episodic rather than consistent and enduring. At the same time, voter participation rates have plummeted in the past four decades, political polarization has increased, and, as political scientist Robert Putnam noted more than a decade ago, "Americans are playing virtually every aspect of the civic game less frequently" (41). And prisons, readers may not be surprised to learn, generally fare far worse than formal education institutions when it comes to education that inspires the kinds of civic engagement that Putnam finds lacking.

Against this backdrop, *Debate and Dialogue in Correctional Settings* offers a way forward not only for those who work with inmates but for all those who hope that educational experiences can play a significant role in nurturing civic and political engagement in children, youth, and adults. By helping participants learn how to draft arguments, take multiple perspectives, engage with others who hold different opinions, and participate in debates, the methods detailed in this book hold significant promise for strengthening democratic thinking and action. First, Diagrammatic Debate and Dialogue (D^3) engenders capacities for thoughtful reflection, respectful disagreement, and constructive criticism—qualities that seem in short supply in our legislative assemblies, in the media, and even at our collective dinner tables. Second, D^3 moves beyond theoretical prescriptions for change; it puts solid step-by-step processes into action in the service of its education goals. Third, D^3 distinguishes itself from traditional debate programs by emphasizing discourse and dialogue rather than competition, winners, and losers.

I witnessed the dialogue and debate program in action when I assisted at a workshop on democracy and education at the Coyote Ridge Corrections Center in Washington State in February 2013. I have seldom had such admiration for educators on the front line. Anyone who has visited correctional facilities in the United States—in particular those serving youth—has seen the heartbreaking despair of the untapped potential of so many incarcerated human beings. And, there are too many of them: 2.3 million, representing the highest incarceration rate in the world. As Massachusetts attorney

Danny Factor pointed out to me, if all the prison inmates in the country could unite and form their own U.S. state, there would be 15 U.S states with smaller populations.

Moreover, whether you view incarceration as a way to be "tough on crime" or as an opportunity for rehabilitation, here's a statistic that should also grab your attention: 95 out of every 100 incarcerated individuals *eventually return to society* (Gorgol & Sponsler)—about half a million each year. A robust democratic society requires its citizens not only to know how to participate effectively in civic affairs but also to be able to entertain multiple perspectives and think critically about contested issues of social and political importance. The program described in this book can help in attaining that goal. Moreover, although under current policies 70–80% of released prisoners are likely to return to prison, prison-based education programs and, in particular, educational activities such as debate and dialogue, have been shown to reduce recidivism by as much as 44 percent (Steurer et al.), further diminishing our reliance on profoundly antidemocratic institutions and strengthening our democratic ones. These activities also respond to alienation and feelings of disengagement by promoting a sense of belonging to both a community of peers and the broader body politic.

Those confined to correctional facilities benefit tremendously from dialogue and debate programs like the one described here, and all of us can benefit from the contribution to society graduates of the program might make once they are free. American entrepreneur Jim Rohn is purported to have said, "If someone is going down the wrong road, he doesn't need motivation to speed him up. What he needs is education to turn him around." Diagrammatic Dialogue and Debate promises to introduce some of our most abandoned and vulnerable populations to multiple perspectives, critical analysis, and the challenges and social benefits of civic engagement. It signals the importance of participation for bringing the democratic ideal closer to reality.

Joel Westheimer
University Research Chair and
Professor of Education
University of Ottawa

References

Gorgol, Laura E., and Brian A. Sponsler. *Unlocking Potential: Results of a National Survey of Postsecondary Education in State Prisons.* Washington, DC: Institute for Higher Education Policy, 2011.

Putnam, Robert D. *Bowling Alone: The Collapse and Revival of American Community.* New York: Simon & Schuster, 2000.

Steurer, Stephen, John Linton, John Nally, and Susan Lockwood. "The Top-Nine Reasons to Increase Correctional Education Programs." *Corrections Today* (August 2010).

INTRODUCTION

The goal of *Debate and Dialogue in Correctional Settings* is to integrate debate into existing educational programming within correctional facilities. This book presents a unique model of debate developed over three years in a correctional facility in southeastern Washington. Diagrammatic Debate and Dialogue (D^3)—pronounced "D three"—is more than a set of principles or specific model of debate. In this book, we present a program that focuses on argumentation, respectful disagreement, constructive criticism, and reflection that can be introduced in a variety of classroom settings through a step-by-step approach. A central assumption of this work is that debate can be an essential classroom tool. We suggest that, instead of focusing solely on competition, point/counterpoint, and the identification and declaration of winners and losers, more attention be paid to how debates can foster reasonable and considered discourse and dialogue.

Our hope is that the resources we have provided and the step-by-step approach that we have used will assist students in developing credible arguments and organizing and presenting them effectively. Properly planned and delivered, this approach to debate can create space for respectful disagreement between and among debaters and their audience. It can teach participants to recognize their own beliefs, promote critical reflection, and allow for more in-depth dialogue among debaters, audiences, and others invited to participate.

Debate has the potential to help students develop specialized skills by modeling and encouraging pro-social interactions, and creating a unique learning activity that can be applied to a number of topics and disciplines. Through debate, students work both alone and in teams and are provided an opportunity to build formal and informal skills associated with self-directed learning and more meaningful education. Debate teaches and fosters reading, summarizing, communication, and critical thinking skills.

A unique aspect of D^3 requires students to acknowledge their own bias as part of drafting arguments, engaging others, and participating in debates. This involves replacing the competitive desire to "win" with a more introspective and self-searching approach to identify reasonable counterarguments, including those with which students may disagree. In this way, debates are seen and experienced, first and foremost, as opportunities to present and consider different information on a wide variety of topics that are based on good-quality sources.

D^3 is unique among debate formats both in prioritizing the potential of debate for promoting dialogue and analyzing arguments and in the use of diagrams, maps, and other visual approaches to assist student learning. These approaches can help students break down complex issues into simpler parts and visualize connections in new ways, including: separating an argument into Pros and Cons; clearly defining the debate topic; planning, organizing, and refining arguments; and keeping track of the arguments made by the opposing team. Used in this way, maps can assist and promote critical thinking throughout the process. Students brainstorm arguments, consider how issues are presented within a debate, and learn to uncover a variety of perspectives that may exist even on difficult and contentious issues. Maps can provide a visual tool to assist students to "see" underlying differences that animate controversial issues. We argue that these issues cannot be resolved unless different perspectives are identified, weighed, considered, and acknowledged.

Debate and Dialogue in Correctional Settings discusses the philosophy and potential of debate in correctional settings. It also provides instructors with ideas to develop practical skills, sample exercises, and a more detailed five-step approach for those interested in using debate in the classroom. As part of our five-step approach, lesson plans and materials are provided that are appropriate for the most common type of correctional education programming, e.g., Adult Basic Education (ABE) and the General Equivalency Diploma (GED) curricula. We have also provided additional materials for more advanced college-level coursework (Associate of Arts [AA] and other undergraduate programs). Our approach can be adapted in correctional facilities offering college-level coursework or used by instructors and volunteers involved in other kinds of post-secondary and higher education programming.

Studies suggest that debate as a teaching tool can spur learning well beyond correctional facilities and is appropriate anywhere that structured, deliberative, evidence-based dialogue is valued. An important strength of debate in the classroom is its adaptability. Instructors can use formal debate and the skills acquired in debating to achieve a variety of educational objectives. For example, they can use the skills underlying debate to teach students how to brainstorm, organize ideas, and consider counterevidence to develop a simple five-paragraph essay. As students progress, the approach provided in this book can be used to build a more advanced college-level argumentative essay.

Instructors can also use debate as an alternative to student presentations and as a means to enliven existing coursework. In short, while structured debate requires preparation and facilitation, debate activities can be used in different ways based on the objectives of the instructor and the level of the class. While we believe our five-step plan to be the most comprehensive approach available, we encourage instructors to experiment with the materials provided to find other ways to incorporate them into their classrooms. Experimentation may include the adoption of our debate model, but it also may simply be the integration of some of the brainstorming activities or approaches to essay writing. As any educator knows, there is no one-size-fits-all policy for every classroom!

The book is organized to link education and pedagogical theory with classroom practice; it also provides some practical ideas about how to implement the model in different educational environments. The first section provides an overview of the goals and five principles that underlie D³. Understanding these is necessary for successfully implementing the program. Section 2 presents some of the challenges incarcerated populations face and explains the value of educational programming for this group. Section 3 discusses the value of debate in education settings and the cognitive and learning skills it can build. Section 4 provides an overview of the D³ model, including the rationale, the role of diagrams, debate, dialogue and debriefing.

Section 5 offers a step-by-step approach to applying the principles of the D³ model to coursework offered in correctional settings. In this section, learning goals and instructor roles are outlined, and debate activities are provided for five levels from ABE 1 and 2, to GED 1 and 2, and finally to AA. For each level, the book provides corresponding materials (located in the Appendix). These may be copied and used by instructors and others in correctional education classrooms and beyond.

Finally, in Section 6, we answer some questions about using debate in correctional settings, including those we have been asked at conferences, workshops, training events, and other venues. This section includes details about our most recent project with Washington State University. While our focus is the correctional classroom, it should be noted that the program has been implemented more broadly at colleges and universities throughout Washington State and the principles have been used as part of other debate programs around the world. While we have stated this above, it bears repeating: debate is a tool, not a cure-all. We hope you will experiment with these materials to find what works best in your classroom.

1.0: GOALS AND PRINCIPLES

Diagrammatic Debate and Dialogue (D³) seeks to foster reason, tolerance, understanding, and model pro-social interactions.[1] The explicit assumption underlying the model is that people of good conscience may reasonably and respectfully disagree on issues of public concern. The D³ model is based on five core principles.

1. **Debates can be used to serve a variety of educational goals.** Debates are based on research, organization, and presentation; debating can be used to meet a variety learning needs and goals. Students should be given class time to prepare and draft debate outline documents and/or diagrams for instructors to review and approve.

2. **Debates should be informational opportunities.** Students review arguments and use visual maps and diagrams to connect related ideas based on credible sources into an argument that addresses the debate topic.

3. **Debates should be conducted in ways that value the skill of presenting a coherent argument.** Success is not solely based on which team wins, but on how well teams present evidence and examples that support their position.

4. **Debates ALWAYS employ respectful discourse and disagreement.** Personal attacks or insults undermine the value and importance of debate and must not be tolerated.

5. **Debaters should interact courteously and answer questions honestly.** Debaters must answer questions from the audience, instructor, or opposing team civilly and acknowledge the best counterarguments before offering concluding remarks.

2.0: EDUCATION IN CORRECTIONAL SETTINGS

. . . the most educationally disadvantaged population in the United States resides in our nation's prisons.[2]

Incarcerated Americans commonly have little formal education. In general, prison populations have high levels of educational challenges and low levels of educational attainment. For example, nearly two in five (39%) fall below the literacy level, compared with one in five (20%) in the general population. Only two-thirds (65%) have high school diplomas or GEDs, compared with more than four in five (82%) of the general population, and only 17 percent have any post-secondary education compared with 51 percent of the general population.[3] Presented visually in Table 1, these statistics suggest education, and especially post-secondary education, remains an important need within correctional settings.

Table 1—Educational Attainment: Incarcerated and General Populations (%)

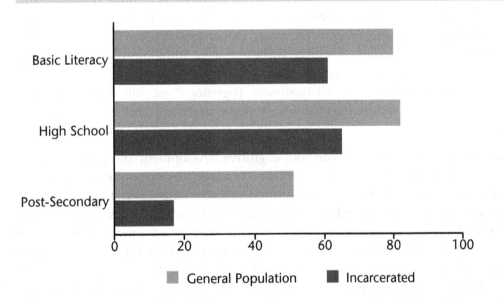

Source: Adapted from D. Brazzell, A. Crayton, D. Mukamal, A. Solomon, and N. Lindahl. 2009. *From the Classroom to the Community: Exploring the Role of Education During Incarceration and Reentry* (Washington, DC: Urban Institute).

Many state prisons throughout the United States recognize the challenges represented by the reality of the populations shown in Table 1 and offer some sort of educational programs. Thirty-two percent offer post-secondary education, 66% offer ABE, and 76% offer adult secondary education, typically through GED programs.[4] Historically the focus has been on literacy, vocational training, and other job-related skills. In recent years, efforts have been made to support other educational goals, including the acquisition of social, relational, and cognitive life skills needed to become an accepted part of and succeed in the general community.[5] Of long-standing interest to educators and others are programs and approaches that foster more rigorous critical thinking skills. These skills are most readily developed through interactive processes, including role-playing, collaborative exercises, and structured deliberation and decision making.

Researchers have discovered that participatory problem-based learning and targeted cognitive behavioral therapies can help participants to develop skills connected to perspective taking and moral reasoning, self-awareness, problem solving and critical thinking.[6] As a result, emergent models of prison programming attempt to target cognitive impairments by:

> . . . changing antisocial attitudes, feelings, and peer associations . . . increasing self-control and self-management skills; replacing . . . aggression with other, more pro-social skills . . . [in] academic, vocational, and other behavioral settings.[7]

Instead of separate programs for education and cognitive behavioral programming, we believe a range of debate activities can be integrated within current correctional education programming. Properly facilitated debate can combine formal traditional academic skill building like research, writing, critical thinking with informal relational abilities and personalized cognitive development associated with perspective taking, moral reasoning, and self-awareness. Together, these skills and abilities can significantly reduce recidivism and improve employment prospects after release from prison.[8]

The principles underlying D[3] can spur cognitive development and promote active learning. Students enjoy the opportunity to research, discuss, present, and defend a range of issues; in doing so, they learn the valuable skills associated with debate. Although many states in the United States still restrict access or limit opportunities for inmates to participate in and benefit from a variety of educational offerings, no better way has been found to reduce the social, economic, and personal costs associated with crime than through effective education (Wheeldon 2011). As we argue in the next section, debate is a valuable tool that supports critical thinking skills and can be used to increase reasoning and interpersonal skills for students of a wide range of abilities.

3.0: WHY DEBATE?

The process of debate offers profound and lasting benefits for individuals, for societies, and for the global community as a whole. With its emphasis on critical thinking, effective communication, independent research and teamwork, debate teaches skills that serve individuals well in school, in the workplace, in political life and in fulfilling their responsibilities as citizens of democratic societies.[9]

D³ builds on widespread support for new approaches to debate to support civic education.[10] Given the increased interest in cognitive behavioral training programs in correctional settings, we argue that debate should be seen as an extension of these programs, with the added value of being part of programming that incarcerated individuals choose, rather than programming that is forced upon them. To achieve the potential for debate as an educational strategy, we must evaluate the challenges of using traditional debate models. D³ has been developed to engender and support specific skills and is most effective when best practices, as outlined below, are integrated into classroom methodologies.

3.1 Debate in the Classroom: Benefits and Lessons

Without doubt, debate in the classroom, wherever located, is of great educational value. Classroom debate lays the groundwork for and strengthens a variety of skills associated with educational success, fosters respectful disagreement, and facilitates student-driven learning. Debate improves student achievement, including higher grade point averages and better scores on required tests such as LSATs and GREs. Overall, those who participate in debate have higher rates of post-graduation employment than others.[11]

Debate has been used in a variety of educational settings and classes and as part of varied coursework (see Figure 1). Because of debate's inherent flexibility, instructors can easily integrate it into many classroom settings using many permutations, depending on factors such as: skill level of the participants, past debate experience, subject matter expertise, learning objectives, and time constraints.[12]

Figure 1—Debate in the Classroom: Some Examples

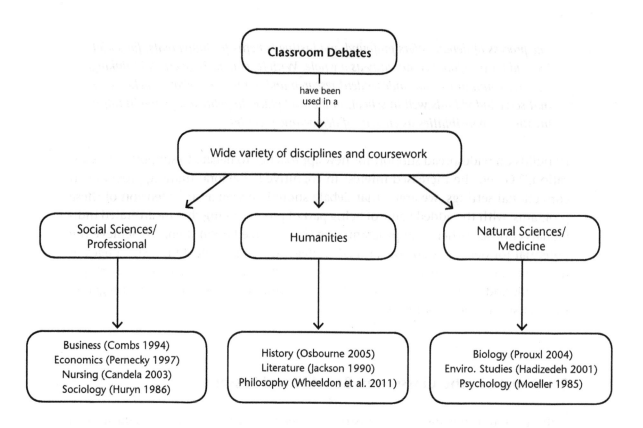

In this book, we expand on the idea that a range of debate activities in the classroom can be used to promote active learning. This approach encourages students to work either collaboratively or independently to research an issue, explore different perspectives on it, and use their research in a debate in front of their class. It requires that student debaters spend time preparing and drafting arguments, while the rest of the class participates in a process to establish the debate rules, brainstorms questions for each side, and considers if their individual positions have changed as a result of the information provided. In our view, debate in the classroom works best when instructors:

- Provide ample in-class time for debate preparation

- Focus on the values and principles of the project throughout

- Ensure class interaction by inviting questions from non-debaters

- Allow the audience to vote by secret ballot for the winning teams

As long as the rules are well-defined, created and communicated clearly, and students have opportunities for different kinds of participation, instructors can structure, organize, and utilize debate in ways that work best for them and their students.[13]

3.2 The Problems with Traditional Debate

Debate activities are commonly thought of in relation to competitive debate, often in the form of well-established debate leagues and competitions. However, this covers only part of how debate can be used . . .[14]

Some aspects of traditional competitive debate[15] are counterproductive to developing moral reasoning, respectful communication skills, and broader educational goals. While the concerns expressed below are especially relevant in correctional settings, they may also apply to many other learning environments.

Too often, traditional debate no longer promotes exchange of information.. Instead, it rewards argumentation skills unique to debate, e.g., cross-examination, speed speaking, and emphasizes winning rather than evaluating arguments. Frequently, competitive debate consists of not only trying to "prove" one position but requires an attempt to "destroy" other positions. To make the most of the potential for classroom debate as a teaching tool, aggressive styles of arguing should be restricted, and debate cannot be seen as a winner-take-all proposition.

While competitive debate undoubtedly has value, the sole focus on developing winning arguments may limit its use in other settings. In our experience, competitive tendencies naturally emerge during a debate. They do not need further encouragement. The energy generated by the potential for a classroom debate should be harnessed for the evaluation of one's own argument, not the deficiencies of one's opponent. When using debate, we suggest instructors avoid the following, which may be a feature of more traditional competitive debates:

Quantity over quality

Quantity over quality refers to a feature of competitive debates in which debaters try to speak as fast as possible. This strategy results from scored competitions in which teams cram as many arguments as possible into a timed speech in the hopes that they can simply outnumber and overwhelm their opponents. In *Wired* magazine, Jay Caspian Kang describes the process:

> The sentences fly out of [the student's] mouth at about 350 words per minute, a good 100 words faster than a well-trained auctioneer, and they will keep flying out at that rate for eight straight minutes. His voice, normally slow and thoughtful, has jumped two octaves. He sounds a bit like [vocalist] Aaron Neville if Aaron Neville had swallowed a cat that had swallowed five pounds of Adderall.[16]

This approach favors the quantity of information over the quality of its communication. This is not consistent with the value of more deliberate and considered speech. Speed-speaking may be one reason why debating, while popular among small groups of highly motivated students, is often unattractive, inaccessible, and unintelligible to others.[17]

Anecdote-based arguments

While teams engage in significant research to build their cases, there is often no requirement for teams to provide their citations or prove that they have rooted their arguments in empirical evidence from credible sources. Instead, unless an opposing team specifically challenges a term, definition, or the evidence provided for an argument, it is judged as "stipulated fact" or accepted for the purposes of the debate. This practice may be connected to competitive debate's prioritization of rhetoric, the ability of a speaker to persuade and/or motivate particular audiences, rather than emphasizing information exchange and analysis.[18]

Even for serious debate scholars and practitioners, the requirement for credibility in debate appears less important than one might assume.[19] Instead of setting high standards in terms of what kind of sources are acceptable, some debate models have acquiesced to the approach of modern political commentary that relies on dubious or unproven statements strenuously and repeatedly presented as fact. We argue that debate works best when the need to define terms and engage in debate based on credible sources and cited evidence are taken seriously. Both sides of the debate should have access to the same sources.

Insults and attacks

Finally, the potential for any debate to devolve into insults and personal attacks is a serious concern. It is a particular problem in correctional settings in which perceived slights, ego, and face-saving are daily concerns. While not all coaches, teams, or debate formats encourage such verbal behavior as part of competitive debate formats, practitioners and facilitators must take seriously the need to promote passionate yet respectful disagreement. To denigrate the work, effort, and attempts of an opposing team is not in line with the stated objectives of promoting respectful discourse and disagreement. Such action is particularly out of place in correctional settings.

If traditional debate models no longer promote the exchange of information and the development of a range of skills associated with critical thinking, existing formats must be adapted or new approaches developed. For debate to reemerge as an essential classroom tool, more attention must be paid to how debates can lead to the dialogue, role-taking, and cognitive development associated with social learning and moral development.

3.3 Debate, Social Learning, and Moral Development

By focusing on social learning and moral development, the D[3] sets itself apart from traditional debate. Social psychologists have determined that positive and negative reinforcement within social structures plays a formative role in the development of social learning—or learning that is influenced by social situations and the interactions that occur.[20] The relevance of social learning to debate is based on the extent to which debate does (or does not) model pro-social interactions. Connected to the concerns presented above about traditional competitive debate, D[3] attempts to model and reinforce ways to disagree respectfully. In short, if the social environment created in the classroom provides the most important learning context for individuals, then more attention must be paid to the strategies we employ.

D[3] also has been developed based on principles of moral development as conceived by psychologist Lawrence Kohlberg, who argues that character formation is a function of specific stages of development. Maturation involves a process by which individuals begin to compare their actions with societal views and expectations. As an individual develops a moral compass, the ways in which people interact on fundamental questions of right and wrong begin to play an increasing role in that person's own decision-making process. As obligations expand beyond the self, the need for individual approval diminishes and decisions are increasingly based on a consideration of a community's values and social experiences. This process is outlined in Figure 2.

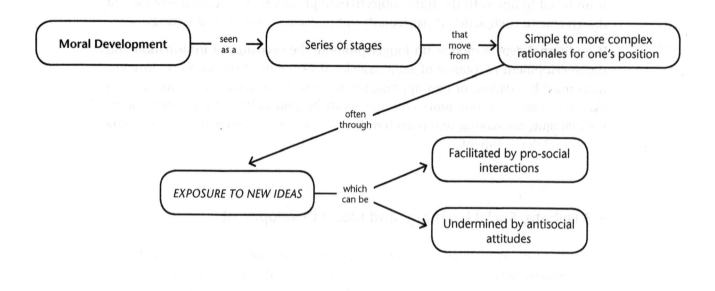

Figure 2—Moral Development, Social Interactions, and Debate

D[3] furthers moral development because it emphasizes exposing students to new ideas and perspectives. During debate, participants may find their views questioned and challenged. The result can be students being motivated to rethink their views or create new, more comprehensive positions. Opportunities to consider other viewpoints can be further strengthened through role-taking or role-playing. When requested to take a position contrary to one personally held, individuals' cognitive processes are activated and stimulated. Through interaction with others and cooperative learning activities, students learn how viewpoints differ and if or how they can be integrated and/or accommodated. Students learn that personal agreement is not required to advance a position.

Instead, the focus is on "being open" to the process of reasoned and reasonable discourse and fidelity to principles rooted in basic respect—even for those with whom you disagree. These interactions work best when they are open and democratic and when problems can be freely discussed and differences reasonably addressed. The value of D[3] is that it provides an instructive and safe place for individuals to challenge one another in pro-social ways. Through this process, individuals develop an increased competence and ability to balance and assess conflicting value-claims, while reconstructing their own arguments with valuable new material and perspectives.[21]

3.4 Skills Development: Variety, Versatility, and Adaptability

D^3 can be used in correctional settings in ways that can promote a range of practical skills associated more broadly with education and learning (see Figure 3).

Figure 3—Using Debate to Develop Education and Social Skills

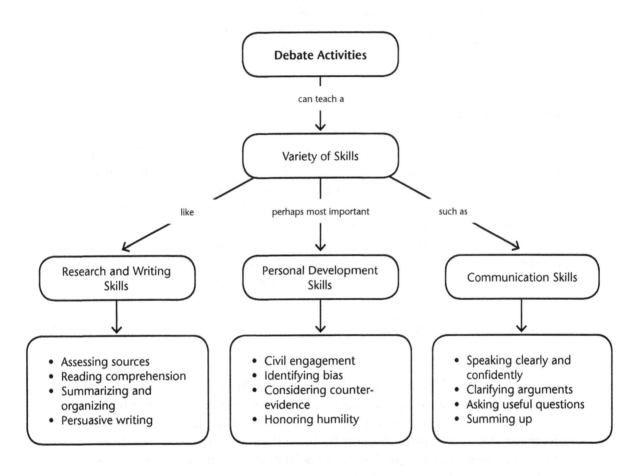

While debate has been shown to foster a number of learning and social skills and results in a variety of important outcomes, our specific interest is how debate can engender and improve academic achievement. For example, participation in debate activities is positively correlated with:

Academic achievement

Debate has been associated with improved literacy, higher graduation rates, and higher scores on reading and writing tests.[22] Classroom debate activities increase subject knowledge and achievement in science, art, and English as a Second Language.[23] Debate also encourages students to delve more deeply into historical events and to understand historical contexts as well as explore differences in viewpoints from the past and the present.[24] D[3] has been designed as a means to reach individuals in correctional settings who have had little exposure to, or success in, traditional learning environments.

Improved critical thinking skills

Participating in debate activities encourages the development of critical thinking skills, including selecting and summarizing evidence; structuring and summing up an argument; identifying counterarguments; and using information gleaned from research to answer relevant questions. A particular strength of D[3] is its focus on ensuring that students evaluate the quality of sources and on encouraging debaters and audience members to identify their own biases and evaluate their own positions. Through a post-debate dialogue, facilitated by the instructor, students have the opportunity to explain which side of the debate they found most convincing.

Improved communication skills

Debate's emphasis on clearly communicating a position helps students gain confidence in otherwise intimidating speaking situations. By researching and preparing, learning a variety of speaking techniques, and working as part of a debate team, students naturally and incrementally gain the ability to communicate their position effectively. Debate also helps students think on their feet, answering questions and revising prepared speeches based on the opposing side's argument. D[3] focuses on the three Cs of communication by encouraging communicating in ways that are:

1. Credible, and based on good sources

2. Consistent, and logically connected with no fallacies

3. Compelling, passionate yet not overbearing, with the ability to recognize the limitations inherent in all arguments

Increased desire for higher education and academic inquiry

Data from U.S. high school debaters reveal that debate participants have a greater desire and commitment to attending college than their non-debating peers. This commitment has been associated with increased interest in the process of research, summarization, and the presentation of divergent views on a number of topics.[25] Our three years of engagement with residents of the Coyote Ridge Corrections Center has convinced us that this focus on and planning for the future is one of the most promising aspects of debate in correctional settings. D^3 can be used in the classroom, as part of debate clubs, and as a means to engage other schools and the broader community outside the prison walls.

4.0: UNDERSTANDING D³

We will never see the sort of civil, thoughtful, inventive debate that enables good public policy making until we inspire the young adults in our midst to pursue it . . .[26]

D³ differs from other models of classroom debate because it encompasses a number of steps—from research and preparation to the actual debate and on to post-debate dialogue. D³ begins with choosing topics and ends when the class (or group) has voted by secret ballot for the winner of the debate and, most important, debriefed the debate. Whether instructors use basic debate activities as part of ABE and GED instruction or hold a more formal debate as part of college-level AA curricula, students are engaging in activities that require them to acknowledge that more than one position exists on a topic.

To implement debate principles and activities in your classroom, instructors must understand how D³ differs from other approaches to debate. In this section, we describe the features and assumptions of D³, the value of maps and diagrams for visual learning, and the steps required in general to organize and facilitate a classroom debate. In each step—from pre-debate preparation to post-debate dialogue—students are challenged to think critically, evaluate their positions, and remain open to dialogue with one another.

4.1 Features and Assumptions of D³

D³ is built on several assumptions. To address the very human inclination to turn every interaction into a competition, our approach attempts to:

- **Balance** the competitive aspects of traditional debate with a more deliberative approach that works to identify credible sources, good arguments, and reasonable counterarguments;

- Encourage **visual** approaches to learning by using maps and diagrams to help teams identify arguments, plan their team argument, and map out their speeches;

- Accept the inherent **limitations** in all arguments by requiring teams to acknowledge the best counterargument on the other side of the debate before a team concludes their presentation.

4.2 Diagrams and Mapping

A unique aspect of the D³ is the use of diagrams, maps, and other visual approaches to assist student learning. Utilizing visual methods in correctional settings is by no means new. Idea maps are often employed to help students brainstorm, break down complex issues into simpler parts, and visualize connections in new ways. This approach can strengthen students' organizational skills and help them to see various components of an argument, such as the main claim, supporting evidence, or practical examples. Visual maps can be used not only to diagram the debate but also the individual speeches in the debate. Their flexibility is what makes them of principal interest to educators and others seeking to reach an audience using multiple means of communication.

Researchers have become increasingly interested in the use of visual tools and techniques.[27] The groundbreaking exploration of the pedagogy of maps and diagrams by Joe Novak and Bob Gowin in education showed that maps are more effective in promoting knowledge retention than attending class lectures, reading, or participating in class discussion. Maps can influence concentration and overall test performance in part because they promote interaction and engagement between the student and the material.[28]

Recent scholarly contributions have attempted to further the use of visual methods in the social sciences. These methods have been shown to be versatile enough to plan research, summarize assumptions, and outline key structural requirements of a research report and to collect qualitative data and mixed-methods data.[29] As part of D³, students must first learn how to map (Appendix 1). Initially, mapping should take the form of brainstorming. Students should create a simple diagram depicting a topic, opinion, or issue. There are no wrong maps or ways to make a map. As long as ideas are visually connected, students can make their own maps in their own way. One strategy to help students learn to map is outlined in Table 2.

Table 2—Making Visual Maps in Five Steps	
Step	Description
1	Make a list of six to eight (6–8) concepts related to a topic of interest
2	Starting in the middle of the page, write the name of the topic and draw two lines outward (one to the left and one to the right)

3	At the end of the lines, use two concepts to show two different perspectives on the topic
4	Now, connect the remaining concepts from your list to the two perspectives to show how each is or is not related
5	Review your map and show it to another student or the instructor. Can someone else understand what your map represents?

Maps may become more complex as students become more comfortable and confident. For example, the map in Figure 4 connects the six concepts: the sun, plant life, people, erosion, clothing, and homes. Appendixes 1a, 1b, and 1c provide map templates for students and instructors to use and adapt as needed.

Figure 4—A Concept Map of the Sun

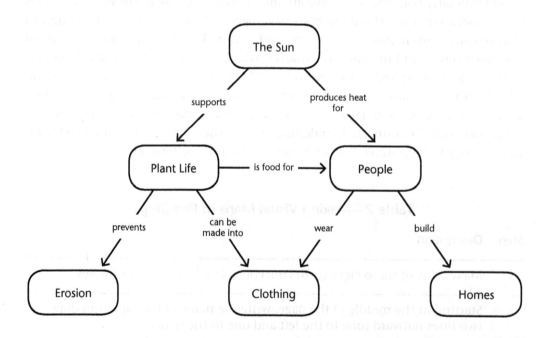

Source: Adapted from J. Wheeldon and J. Faubert. 2009. "Framing Experience: Concept Maps, Mind Maps, and Data Collection in Qualitative Research," *International Journal of Qualitative Methods* 8, no. 3: 68–83.

Students using D³ utilize visual maps to brainstorm a variety of arguments and examples (Pro and Con) on an issue of interest. Take, for example, the statement "Football is a better sport than baseball." Figure 5 provides one way to map some possible arguments for and against this proposition. This example provides arguments for baseball instead of arguments against football—it is but one approach, however. There are others.

Figure 5—Pro/Con Idea Map

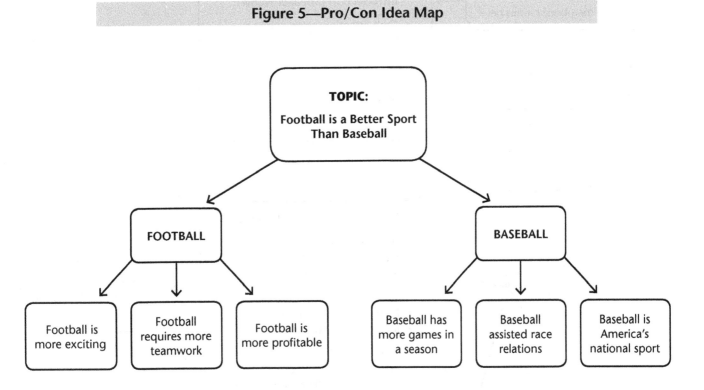

Once students are familiar with the process, they can create more elaborate and detailed maps. They can outline a debate so that they can visualize their team's case and remind themselves of each member's role and responsibilities (see Figure 6). Student debaters can then use a map to prepare their speeches in more detail, setting out their arguments and connecting claims and evidence (see Figure 7, also provided in Appendix 20). These maps also serve as a quick review before a debater presents her speech.

Figure 6—Template of a Team's Debate Map

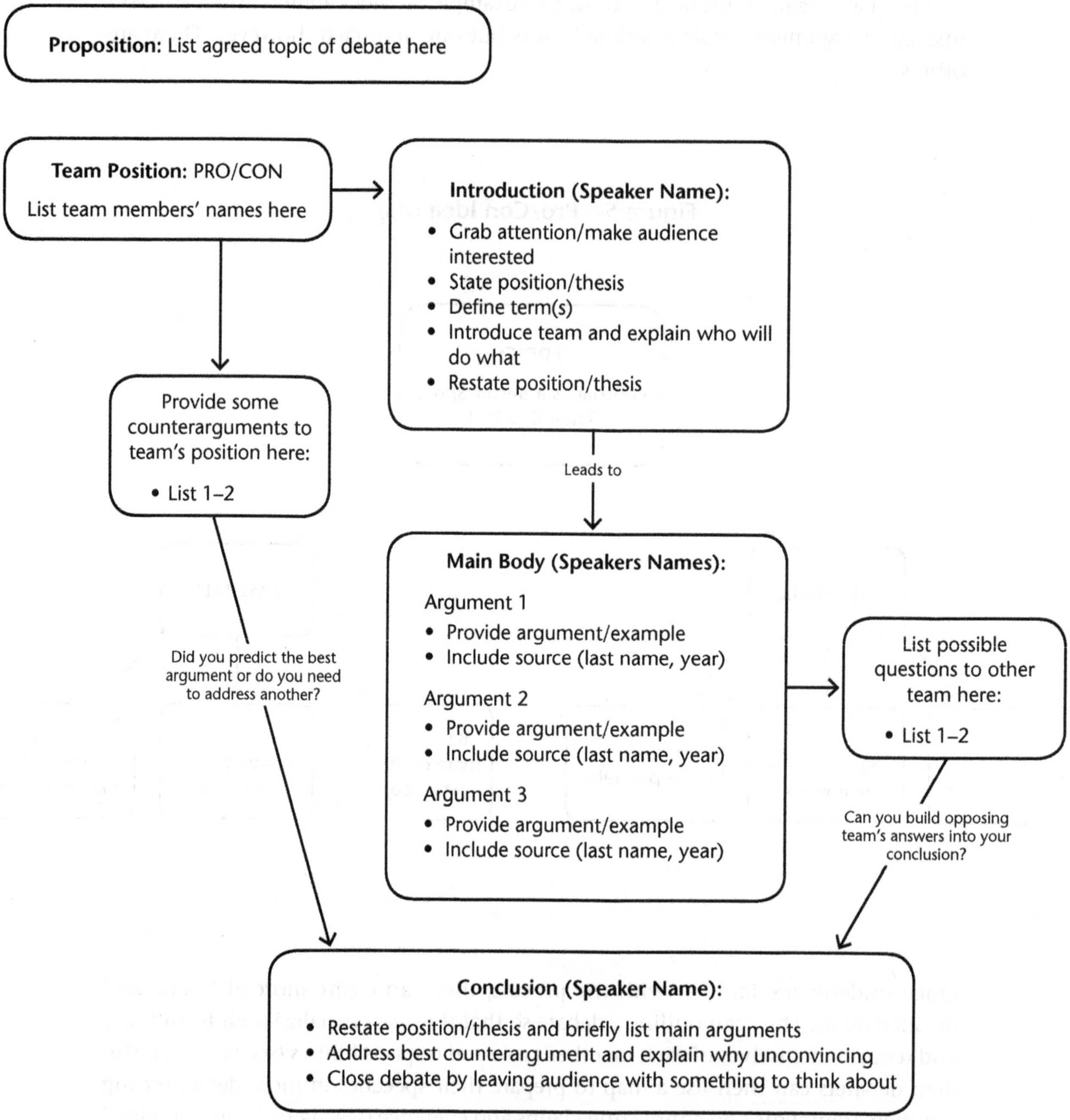

Proposition: List agreed topic of debate here

Team Position: PRO/CON

List team members' names here

Introduction (Speaker Name):
- Grab attention/make audience interested
- State position/thesis
- Define term(s)
- Introduce team and explain who will do what
- Restate position/thesis

Provide some counterarguments to team's position here:
- List 1–2

Did you predict the best argument or do you need to address another?

Leads to

Main Body (Speakers Names):

Argument 1
- Provide argument/example
- Include source (last name, year)

Argument 2
- Provide argument/example
- Include source (last name, year)

Argument 3
- Provide argument/example
- Include source (last name, year)

List possible questions to other team here:
- List 1–2

Can you build opposing team's answers into your conclusion?

Conclusion (Speaker Name):
- Restate position/thesis and briefly list main arguments
- Address best counterargument and explain why unconvincing
- Close debate by leaving audience with something to think about

Figure 7—Main Elements of a Speech

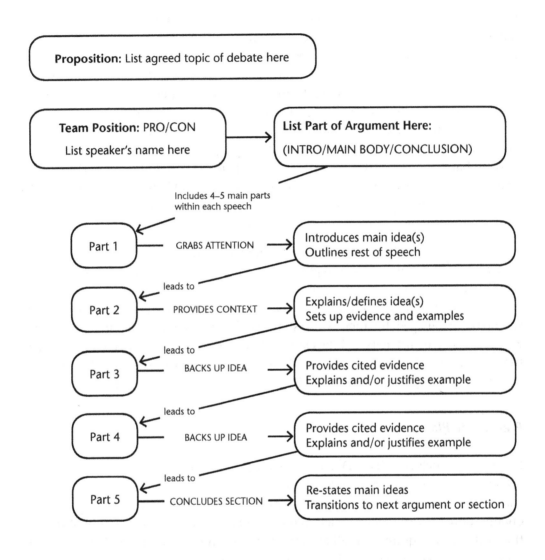

Proposition: List agreed topic of debate here

Team Position: PRO/CON
List speaker's name here

List Part of Argument Here:
(INTRO/MAIN BODY/CONCLUSION)

Includes 4–5 main parts within each speech

Part 1 — GRABS ATTENTION → Introduces main idea(s)
Outlines rest of speech

leads to

Part 2 — PROVIDES CONTEXT → Explains/defines idea(s)
Sets up evidence and examples

leads to

Part 3 — BACKS UP IDEA → Provides cited evidence
Explains and/or justifies example

leads to

Part 4 — BACKS UP IDEA → Provides cited evidence
Explains and/or justifies example

leads to

Part 5 — CONCLUDES SECTION → Re-states main ideas
Transitions to next argument or section

4.3 Debates and Dialogue

As we have discussed, D^3 puts greater emphasis on the potential for debate to facilitate dialogue and promote learning rather than on some of debate's traditional competitive characteristics. It seeks to harness the many benefits of student debate in the classroom and provide an example of and experience with a deliberative process. D^3 is designed to encourage participants and audience members to carefully consider different arguments before asserting a position on the topic. Students often become excited about the dramatic possibilities of debate events and the potential to command the attention of a room. They will naturally engage in competitive and sometimes boastful banter. Some of this is normal, but instructors should be wary. The goal of D^3 is to showcase how debate can help clarify thought and help individuals come to considered conclusions rather than debate being the competitive demonstration of research, organization, and communication skills.

Instructors can assist by providing the principles of D^3 (Appendix 15) and reminding the class that the goal is to expand perspectives and consider new arguments. Instructors should facilitate their classes' movement from the debate to further discussions with others—and sometimes further debates. These discussions and considerations should be encouraged. Instructors also should be clear that while student performance will be assessed by teachers and the class itself, D^3 works best when debaters recognize their role as one of attempting to provide and provoke more in-depth and considered discussion among the audience. The focus is definitely not on which team "wins."

Pre-Debate Planning

Like other models of debate, D^3 requires teams to conduct research, analyze sources, evaluate and organize arguments, and consider how their arguments and position should be delivered. Central to D^3 is the assumption that debates must be based on quality sources. While some models of debate focus more on the credibility of sources than others, D^3 requires that all arguments be based on credible academic sources, properly cited, and integrated into speeches. Focusing on sources and citations can allow instructors to explore concepts such as the difference between primary and secondary sources, the process of peer review, and the problems with plagiarism.

Once good sources are identified and summarized, students can turn their attention to how different arguments might be organized into a coherent team position on a topic of interest. Diagrams and maps can assist individual students and teams to outline and organize their arguments (first separately and then together) to attempt to tailor arguments for maximum impact. One approach we have used is to encourage students to think about the differences and relative strengths and weaknesses of three kinds of arguments as presented in Figure 8.

These include:

1. Arguments of fact, which can be empirically proved or disproved

2. Arguments of value, which are based on a moral or ethical claim

3. Arguments of policy, which advance a specific and logically connected proposal

Figure 8—Connecting Arguments of Fact, Value, and Policy

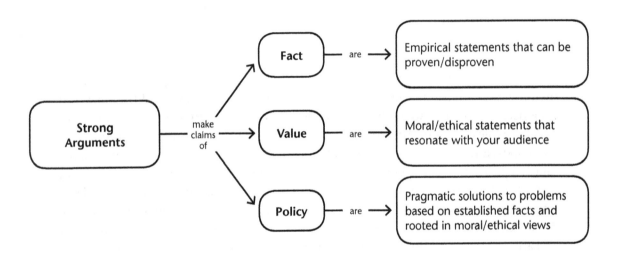

Teams also develop possible questions to pose to the opposing team, try to predict counterarguments, and consider how these counterarguments might be addressed.

As discussed above, a unique feature of D³ is the use of visual maps to supplement the written debate outline document. Diagrams, maps of team positions, and individual student speeches serve as useful visual aids. Instructors should require that these documents include the sources used, visually demonstrate the logic of their arguments, and provide interesting examples, questions for the other side, or possible replies to predicted questions. Instructors should allow time for the class to do group work, and require these outline documents *before* debates begin.

As instructors review the outline documents provided by each team, it can be useful to quiz debate participants on who is doing which part of the debate and what arguments, evidence, and examples they will use in the class before the debate. Make sure everyone is on the same page, has practiced their speech, and is prepared. It is normal for some students to be nervous. Remind these students that genuine effort will be noted and that, as long as they have tried to incorporate credible evidence into a logical argument, they will be fine. Sometimes success is simply a matter of confronting situations that make us nervous. Provide each team 15 minutes at the beginning of the debate class to finalize their strategy (Appendix 19). This strategy should be followed in individual speeches (Appendix 20). Instructors can assist students by encouraging them to develop versions of the same map—one should be handed in and one can be used by the student himself during the debate if they wish. The instructor can use the submitted maps to assess student learning and quickly offer suggestions and corrections.

D³ Debates

A central aspect of D³ is a commitment by debaters to the principles and values of the program. No debate should proceed unless the class has reviewed the roles and responsibilities chart (Appendix 21), and debaters have agreed to abide by the values and principles listed in Appendix 15. D³ uses a three-part structure—introduction, main body, and conclusion—designed to focus the debate squarely on the arguments for each position, their presentation, and their communication. In the introduction, teams first focus on grabbing the audience's attention, defining their terms, and setting forth the approach they will use to make their case. In the main body of the debate, each team then presents evidence and examples based on their stated position and answers questions in a manner consistent with their research and their position.

In the conclusion, the team's main argument is briefly restated and their case summarized. Whoever is delivering the conclusion must also acknowledge the best argument on the other side. Instructors can assist by suggesting language like: "Our friends have made several useful points. Perhaps their strongest argument is . . . " Once acknowledged, problems or limitations with that argument should be discussed. The team should conclude their part of the debate with a clear and concise statement about why their team's argument/solution should be chosen. Students should be provided with the main roles and responsibilities of each section long before the debate to allow them time to properly prepare (see Table 3, also provided in Appendix 18).

Table 3—D³ Debate Format

Section	Roles and Responsibilities
Introduction (Pro) (2–3 Mins)	• Define the topic • Present the PRO team's position • Outline briefly what the team will talk about
Introduction (Con) (2–3 Mins)	• Accept or offer alternative definition • Present the CON team's position • Outline briefly what the team will present
Main Body (Pro) (5–7 Mins)	• Reaffirm the PRO team's position • Provide evidence/arguments/examples that support team's position • Usually 2–3 separate points are made here
Main Body (Con) (5–7 Mins)	• Reaffirm the CON team's position • Provide evidence/arguments/examples that support team's position • Usually 2–3 separate points are made here
Questions (5–7 Mins)	• PRO asks CON 1 question • CON asks PRO 1 question • Chair selects 1–2 audience questions per team
Conclusion (Pro) (3–4 Mins)	• Restate position • Present a summary of case • Acknowledge and answer best counterargument • Conclude case for their team

Conclusion (Con) (3–4 Mins)	• Restate position
	• Present a summary of case
	• Acknowledge and answer best counterargument
	• Conclude case for their team

D³ emphasizes constructing arguments rather than destroying them. For example, after the Pro team makes their 2–3 best arguments in favor of the proposition, Con offers their 2–3 best arguments against the proposition. In a traditional debate, the Con team would focus not on building an alternate case but, instead, on trying to show why one element of the Pro case is confused or incorrect. This can result in an unproductive back-and-forth that can easily lead one or both debate teams to violate the core principles outlined in Section 1. By asking each team to present their best possible case and using the question-and-answer period to identify possible problems with each position, D³ forces participants to analyze the issue first and present the best possible case *before* critiquing their opponents.

D³ also stresses respectful dialogue. By requiring each team to acknowledge and answer their opponent's best argument, D³ ensures that all debaters explicitly recognize the strengths of each team's case. This is valuable to debaters because the process of thinking through counterarguments requires that debate teams begin to consider not only the strengths of their own case but also the possible objections or counterarguments the other side might make. Thus, D³ involves deep introspection. As students' exposure to debate principles and activities grows, so, too, does their appreciation of the complexity of many issues. Students can be exposed to ideas they have never thought about and are required through D³ to acknowledge positions with which they may not personally agree. This aspect of D³ is also valuable for the debate audience. When teams fail, forget, or refuse to acknowledge counterevidence, the audience may conclude that a team has not properly prepared and/or adhered to the model's core principles. This may be a factor in their vote.

D³ Post-Debate Dialogue

While students often consider the debate as the main attraction and the culmination of their efforts, instructors may view the post-debate dialogue as equally or even more important. Post-debate dialogue is another unique feature of D³ and offers a useful means for students to review the arguments made, evaluate their own opinions, and consider the complexity associated with different perspectives.

Following the debate and before announcing the winner, the audience should show their appreciation for the debaters' effort by clapping. Students can then vote by secret ballot to determine which side won the debate; writing "Pro" or "Con" on a small slip of paper should suffice. Students may vote for the team they personally agree with or for the team they thought had the best arguments. In either case the instructor should urge them to consider why they are voting the way they are. The instructor should vote if there is an even number of audience members.

As the ballots are being collected and tallied, the instructor should debrief with the class. They may ask general questions such as:

- What was the best argument made by each side in the debate?

- What was the best answer to a question?

- Did people vote based on their personal opinion or on how well each team presented their side of the debate?

- Would students have changed their vote if they had voted for best arguments, instead of the side they personally agreed with?

Properly facilitated, post-debate dialogue gives the class as a whole the opportunity to reflect on what they heard from debaters and what they have learned from others and themselves. By reflecting on how they approached their own personal decision-making process, students are invited to consider if, how, and/or why they may have changed their position or perspective. It also showcases in a very practical way how respectful debate can promote and lead to more and more in-depth dialogue on specific topics.

Participation, Assessment, and How to Grade Debates

An additional strength of D^3 is the explicit focus on participation by the entire class. Whether students help select topics, assist with research, present speeches as part of the formal debate, or simply participate as an audience member, they all have an important role. One approach we have used is inviting GED classes to participate as the audience for AA debates. This can be challenging for AA students, who must adjust their communication of arguments to reach students at the beginning of their academic careers. It also exposes GED students to the more in-depth arguments that are a typical feature of AA coursework. Mixing classes in this way may offer students and staff a glimpse of their shared purpose and can assist in building bridges between and among instructors and students alike. Table 4 (also provided as Appendix 21) sets out key roles and responsibilities for those who participate, whether as a Chair or Moderator, Debater, or Audience Member.

Table 4—Roles and Responsibilities

Chairs	Debaters	Audience
Collect outline documents	Prepare arguments and connect individual speeches to tell a story	Keep an open mind
Review time for speeches	Draft outline documents	Write down best arguments
Manage debate	Prepare/Predict possible questions	Prepare short, clear questions
Collect and ask audience questions	Deliver 2-minute speeches	Watch to ensure each team debates respectfully and acknowledges counterarguments
Tally votes	Stay respectful at all times and answer ALL questions honestly	Vote on debate winner, respond to questions, engage in classroom dialogue

D^3 has also been developed with a specific view of assessment. Traditionally, judges determine debate winners; D^3, in contrast, has the audience decide the winner by a secret ballot vote. However, D^3 acknowledges that for certain issues and among certain audiences, some teams may have an advantage. Thus, while the class determines the winning team, victory is less important than the quality of the arguments presented. This may be at odds with more competitive formats that focus on "winners" and "losers." It is, however, in line with our view that debate can be used as a vehicle to allow the class to evaluate academic sources, consider the arguments presented, and reflect on the role of their own preconceived notions. An example may be useful here.

We have had classes that debate whether the criminal justice system should focus more on punishment or on rehabilitation. In a prison environment, the team arguing in favor of rehabilitation has a built-in advantage even before the presentation of the first argument. D^3 allows for the possibility that while the team that argues for punishment can "lose the debate," they may present better arguments. As a result, they may receive higher scores on the debate assessment completed by the instructor than the "winning" team that got more audience votes. This approach can lead to in-class discussions about the difference between "winning" a debate (vote) and presenting the best possible case for one's position—and why these might not always be the same. Another key element is the extent to which debaters remained respectful throughout the debate. Instructors must be aware that when the principles of D^3 are compromised, the pedagogical value of the model is significantly reduced.

Instructors should consider which elements they want to focus on before assessing and/or grading student performance. The specific elements should be provided to students *before* the debate. While the audience votes for the team they thought "won," the debate, instructors should focus on the quality of work, the questions asked of the other side, and the answers each team provided to such questions. Instructors might also consider verbal and non-verbal skills (see Appendixes 22 & 23) as well as other elements outlined in the assessment tool provided in Appendix 24.

5.0: FIVE STEPS TO INTEGRATE DEBATE INTO THE CLASSROOM

As described in Section 4, D³ involves a new debate format that instructors can use to teach and reinforce a variety of skills associated with debate. This approach is, however, more than simply a revised debate format. In this section, we present how debate can be introduced to different classes based on a five-step process and used alongside common correctional education programming from Adult Basic Education to General Education Diploma and Associate of Arts curricula. To mirror the varied levels of educational experience common in one correctional classroom, we present five steps that have been structured and developed for different learners. We suggest that you start all students at the first step to allow them to get comfortable with using diagrams to brainstorm, create Pro/Con tables, and clearly articulate a position. Table 5 provides an overview of our step-by-step approach.

Table 5—A Five-Level Approach to Integrate Debate into the Classroom

Step	Level	Activity	Instructor Role	Output
1	Beginner (ABE 1)	Using Idea Maps to brainstorm topics	Instructor leads initial discussion	1 collective map by instructor 1 personal map by student
2	Beginner (ABE 2)	From brainstorming to Pro/Con tables	Instructor assists construction of tables/maps	1 table per student 1 position map per student
3	Intermediate (GED 1)	Understanding maps, critical reflection, and education plans	Instructor assists students to complete map, table, and plan	In (3–4) small groups output is 1 table per group 1 Barriers and Solutions Table per student 1 education plan per student

4	Intermediate (GED 2)	Organize, draft, revise and finalize 5-paragraph essays	Instructor provides feedback and organizes student peer review	Based on one-on-one meetings each student develops an essay
				Each student peer reviews another's essay
5	Advanced (AA)	Debate and dialogue	Instructor facilitates student debate	Whole class participates in D^3 debate

We believe debate activities may have the greatest impact in the ABE/GED classroom. A number of skills associated with debate can be applied to existing ABE/GED course-work in steps one through four. Students can use idea maps to brainstorm issues, using Pro/Con tables to organize arguments, develop education plans, and use skills acquired together to construct a five-paragraph GED essay. In the full debate model, outlined in Step 5, these skills are integrated to research, conduct, and reflect on a class debate. We suggest that students be introduced to D^3 gradually and in a manner consistent with their educational level and abilities. When introduced deliberately, debate activities can allow beginner-level students to feel comfortable expressing and expanding their opinions and help them to begin to think about issues employing the Pro/Con format. What follows are step-by-step procedures for introducing debate into the correctional classroom.

5.1 Step 1—Using Idea Maps to Brainstorm Topics (ABE 1)

Goals for students:

- Students are introduced to brainstorming in a positive environment that fosters active listening within the classroom

- Students can make a map based on the provided instructions

- Students are introduced to Pro/Con mapping in a way that values all suggestions

Materials:

Appendix 1: Making a Map

Appendix 2: Pro/Con Map

The main goal of Step 1 is for students to learn to make idea maps to brainstorm topics. This requires the instructor to support open brainstorming and support students in identifying various unique ideas and making connections between them instead of trying to rank or limit them. At this stage, all (or most) ideas are acceptable. Encourage students to make a map of their preferences, focused on their likes and dislikes using the process in Table 6 and based on the examples provided in Appendix 1.

Table 6—Making Visual Maps in Five Steps	
Step	Description
1	Make a list of six-to-eight (6–8) concepts related to a topic of interest
2	Starting in the middle of the page, write the name of the topic and draw two lines outward (one to the left and one to the right)
3	At the end of the lines, use two concepts to show two different perspectives on the topic
4	Now connect the remaining concepts from your list to the two perspectives to show how each is or is not related
5	Review your map and show it to another student or the instructor. Does he understand what your map represents?

For example, students could be asked to make a map of things they like and things they dislike (see, for example, Figure 9).

Figure 9—Mapping Likes and Dislikes

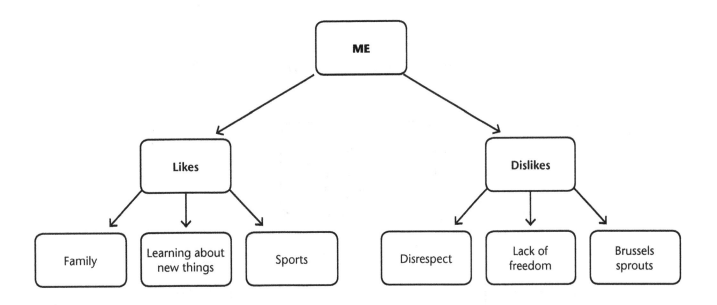

Instructors can make a list of the broad of common likes and dislikes identified by students. They can then make a collaborative class map by voting on which of the common likes/dislikes on the board are the most pervasive. Another activity might include having students exchange their maps and then make a second map comparing and contrasting their maps with their partner's. Instructors must be alert for inappropriate verbal expression and work to ensure that students listen to one another and refrain from possible disruptive, disrespectful, or thoughtless remarks.

As students become more comfortable mapping their ideas, instructors can explore how to use maps to present Pro/Con positions. Utilizing Appendix 2: Pro/Con Map, students should choose topics to map. These will vary and might include a sport or team, an issue in the news, or something more personal such as the benefit of getting an education.

Instructors must be sure to assist students in choosing a topic and also work to ensure that students do not feel that their ideas are weak or uninteresting. Students should be reminded that the goal, as such, isn't to choose a compelling topic, but, rather, acquiring the skills to brainstorm, organize, and map their ideas. At this stage, student choice of topic should be prioritized and all ideas placed on the map. The map

Is Football a Better Sport than Baseball?, which we introduced in Section 4, serves as a useful example to share as students begin to select their own topics.

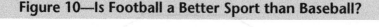

Figure 10—Is Football a Better Sport than Baseball?

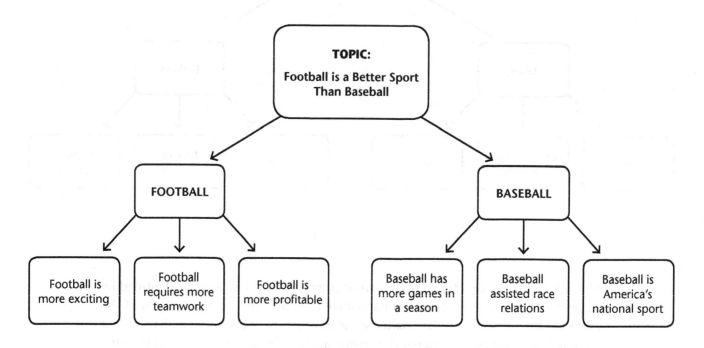

The next step involves supporting students in developing Pro/Con maps based on topics provided by the instructor. Initially, in response to the question, "Should seatbelt laws be enforced?" students might argue that seatbelts save lives, but counter that seatbelts may endanger a driver if she were entangled by her seatbelt in an accident. Both points would be valid and should be placed on the appropriate side of the Pro/Con map. Soon, students can add other, more sophisticated arguments (see Figure 11). Students can follow along as ideas are placed in Pro or Con sides of the argument and offer their opinions.

Figure 11—Mapping "Should Seatbelt Laws Be Enforced?

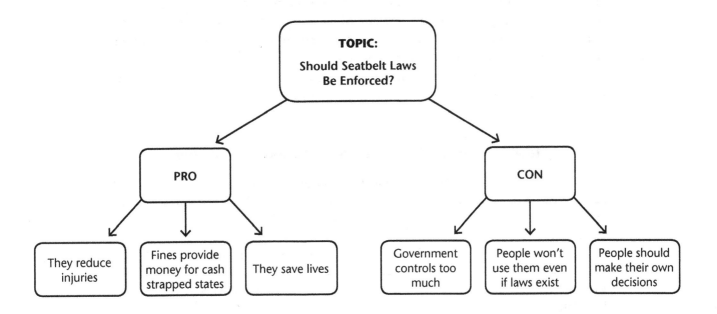

5.2 Step 2—From Brainstorming to Pro/Con Tables (ABE 2)

Goals for students:

- Students develop Pro/Con tables based on Pro/Con maps

- Students take a position based on a Pro/Con table and express why one side of the table is stronger than the other

- Students begin to weigh and balance different arguments and perspectives before arriving at their position

Materials:

Appendix 2: Pro/Con Map

Appendix 3: Pro/Con Table

Appendix 4: Mapping Your Position

The main goal of Step 2 is for students to learn to make Pro/Con tables based on Pro/Con maps introduced in Step 1. Using these tables is a simple way to organize and group the Pro/Con ideas developed in an idea map. When creating a Pro/Con table, students focus on providing the opposite of each argument. If a student mentions a specific argument in support of an issue, he or she must offer a counterargument. For example, if the issue were whether television is good for children, a "Pro" might be that it provides educational programs, whereas the "Con" would be that TV contains too much violence. Table 7 provides an example.

Table 7—Pro/Con Table: Television Is Good for Children

ISSUE: IS TELEVISION GOOD FOR CHILDREN?

Pro	Con
TV is educational	TV contains too much violence
Kids can learn letters, numbers, language	Kids learn that violence solves problems
Helps stimulate imagination, creativity	Desensitizes kids through visual input with little context
Can involve parents	TV used as a babysitter
Features history, geography, science	Focus on entertainment programs, not learning
Examples: Programs like *Sesame Street, Dora, National Geographic, Nova, Discovery* can assist learning	Examples: Programs like *Beavis & Butthead, Simpsons, South Park* are inappropriate for younger viewers

Once students have created their tables, they can use Appendix 4: Mapping Your Position to outline their personal position on a topic. Using the TV example in Table 7, students can make a map that begins with the topic, lists their position, and connects three arguments starting with the strongest. Figure 12 (also provided in Appendix 4) shows how a position could be mapped. Have students use the box numbered 1 for the strongest argument; 2 for the second; and 3 for the third strongest. The ability to assess arguments is a valuable skill that will assist students as they develop critical thinking skills.

Figure 12—Mapping Your Position

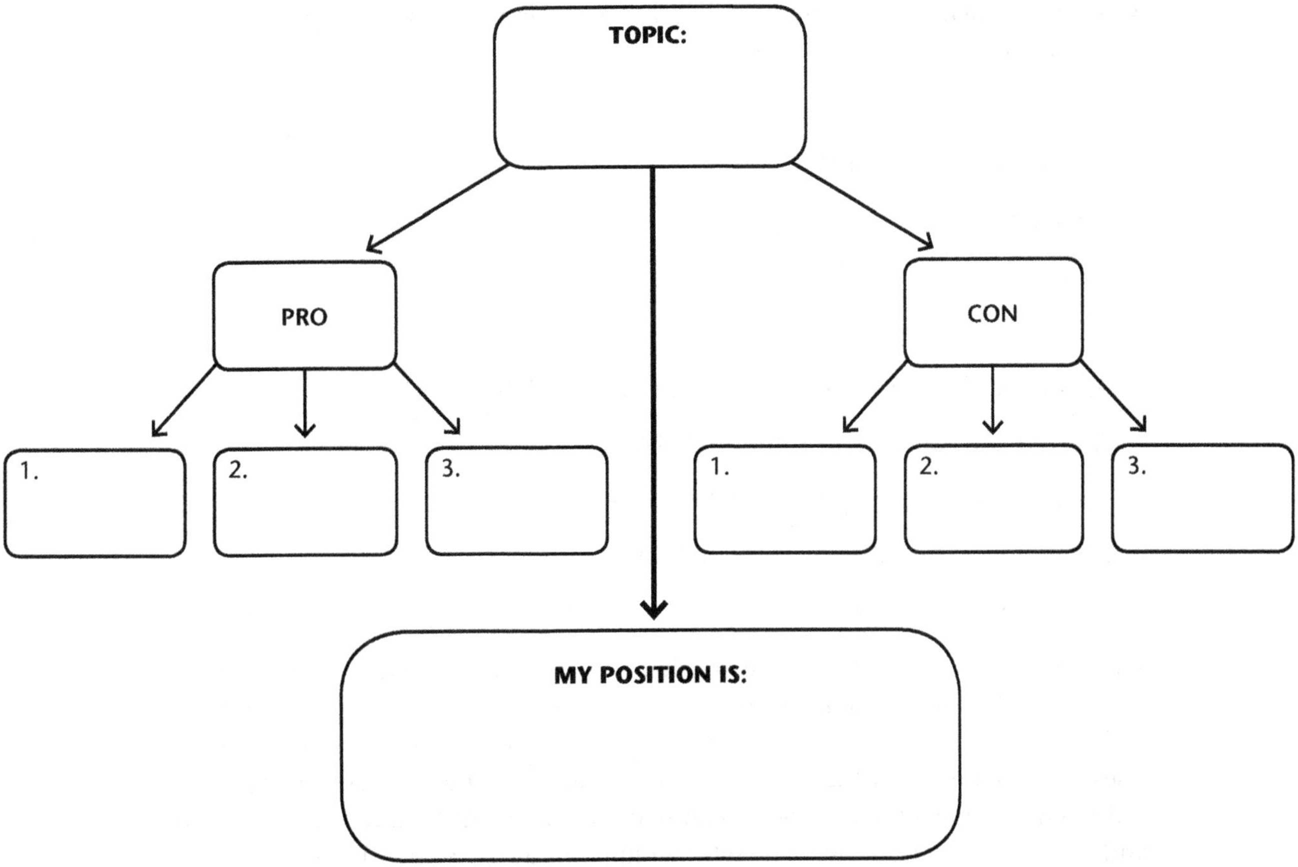

```
                          ┌──────────────────┐
                          │      TOPIC:       │
                          └──────────────────┘
              ┌──────────────────┼──────────────────┐
         ┌─────────┐                          ┌─────────┐
         │   PRO    │                          │   CON    │
         └─────────┘                          └─────────┘
      ┌────┬────┬────┐                      ┌────┬────┬────┐
   ┌─────┐┌─────┐┌─────┐              ┌─────┐┌─────┐┌─────┐
   │ 1.  ││ 2.  ││ 3.  │              │ 1.  ││ 2.  ││ 3.  │
   └─────┘└─────┘└─────┘              └─────┘└─────┘└─────┘

                   ┌──────────────────────────┐
                   │     MY POSITION IS:        │
                   │                            │
                   └──────────────────────────┘
```

5.3 Step 3—Maps, Critical Reflection, and Education Plan

Goals for students:

- Students use maps to brainstorm, organize ideas, and visually present arguments by reviewing steps 1 and 2

- Students can critically reflect on their past education, identify present barriers, and devise strategies for future educational achievement

- Students are introduced to five-paragraph essay model and develop a personalized education plan

Materials:

Appendix 1: Making a Map

Appendix 2: Pro/Con Map

Appendix 3: Pro/Con Table

Appendix 4: Mapping Your Position

Appendix 5: Mapping Education and Learning Skills

Appendix 6: Barriers and Solutions Table

Appendix 7: 5-Paragraph Personal Education Plan

Appendix 8: The GED 5-Paragraph Essay

Appendix 9: 5-Paragraph Essays—Section-by-Section

The main goal of Step 3 is to ensure that students understand mapping and diagrams and their use to brainstorm, organize ideas, and visually present arguments. As some students may test into a GED class without being exposed to the ABE exercises described in Steps 1 and 2, instructors should use the exercises in Appendixes 1–4 to ensure that all new students can make a map, identify differing perspectives, and articulate why they view one set of arguments as more convincing. In addition to these core skills, Step 3 requires students to engage in more critical reflection. One approach is for instructors to advise students to reflect on their educational experience to date using Appendix 5: Mapping Education and Learning Skills. In mapping their educational histories, students should include other kinds of education, such as trades or computer skills, or past experiences that they feel have helped them learn something valuable.

Students who complete this visual exercise[30] about their own history can then engage in critical reflection by using Table 8 (also provided as Appendix 6). Based on their maps, students should identify past or present barriers to educational achievement and ways (solutions) to overcome such barriers. This table should include one column for Barriers, one column for Solutions, and should focus on ways to overcome these barriers. Once these are created, instructors can have students make a new map of their educational strategy based on their personal Barriers and Solutions table.

Table 8—Identifying Barriers and Finding Solutions Based on Educational History	
Barrier	Solution
Don't like to read	Find books I actually like
Can't remember concepts	Make more maps

Instructors can share the maps and tables of other students as appropriate and with permission. Instructors may use common barriers and solutions identified by students to develop a class code of conduct that all can agree on. These rules and responsibilities can guide instructor-student interactions. Instructors can assist by sharing their expectations with their students and, at the end of the semester, have students reflect on their success and the challenges they faced in overcoming the obstacles they had identified.

Maps and plans can also be used to assist students constructing a five-paragraph education plan. These should be designed and developed based on discussions with the instructor. Once students can reflect on their past educational experiences and identify possible barriers to and solutions for future success, instructors can encourage them to develop a personal education plan using Table 9 (also provided as Appendix 7). Using the table, students can transfer ideas that emerged from the education history map (Appendix 5) and Barriers and Solutions table (Appendix 6) into personal statements of educational intent. This activity also serves to introduce students to the five-paragraph format. Bulleted outlines can be used for early drafts. These outlines can be developed into full sentences as each student progresses.

Table 9—Structure for 5-Paragraph Education Plan

Paragraph Structure	Contains Statements that	Examples
Introductory Paragraph	• Explain why education is important to the student	• Prove to myself I can succeed; get a better job; go to college
	• Provide past education challenges	• Difficult home life; drug use; gang activity; just not ready
	• State a personal education goal	• Complete GED; read (and understand) textbooks
First Body Paragraph	• Outline one strategy to achieve goal	• Develop education plan based on my strengths and weaknesses
	• Provide examples or related ideas	• Strength: like to read • Weakness: writing skills
Second Body Paragraph	• Outline second strategy to achieve goal	• Set aside time every night to work on my assignments
	• Provide examples or related ideas	• Need to find time between job and program
Third Body Paragraph	• Provide biggest past education barrier or challenge	• Friends don't take education seriously • Worried my writing skills are not good enough
	• Provide possible solution to this barrier	• Find new people to work with who want to succeed • Find a writing guide or resource to help me improve
Concluding Paragraph	• Restate personal education goal	• Complete GED; read (and understand) textbooks
	• Discuss strategies to attain goal and overcome barriers	• Develop plan; set aside time every night; find more motivated friends; read writing guide and complete exercises

5.4 Step 4—Organize, Revise, and Finalize Argumentative Essays (GED 2)

Goals for students:

- Students draft a five-paragraph essay based on a topic identified in class materials

- Students accept suggestions and constructive criticism from instructors and revise their drafts to address instructor comments

- Students show their work to other students, explain the process they used to create their essay, and finalize their essay based on comments

Materials:

Appendix 4: Mapping Your Position

Appendix 8: The GED 5-Paragraph Essay

Appendix 9: 5-Paragraph Essays—Section-by-Section

Appendix 10: Exploring Essay Topics Using Pro/Con Tables

Appendix 11: Drafting Essay Topics Using Maps

Appendix 12: GED Essay Grading Rubric

The main goal of Step 4 is for students to learn how to draft and outline a five-paragraph essay. This requires several steps. Instructors can assist progression by reminding students that writing essays involves first organizing their arguments. A number of revisions may be necessary to ensure they are making good and clear arguments.

Instructors should first introduce the five-paragraph essay by comparing it to the five-paragraph personal education plan students completed in Step 3. In a five-paragraph essay, each section has a specific goal. Consulting Appendix 8: Lesson Plan: The 5-Paragraph Essay, instructors may use any resource that provides essay topic examples. To assist instructors, we have compiled some examples from existing GED coursework in Appendix 10: Exploring Essay Topics Using Pro/Con Tables and in Appendix 11: Drafting Essays Using Maps. For each topic, students should be encouraged to brainstorm, map arguments, create Pro/Con tables, and develop position maps.

Once these have been created, the information from the Pro/Con tables can be used to develop a five-paragraph essay. Instructors can provide Appendix 9: 5-Paragraph Essay—Section-by-Section to help students understand how each of the five sections advances an argument. Table 10 provides the structure for a five-paragraph essay and includes an example that instructors may employ to assist students in drafting their essays.

Table 10—Structure of a 5-Paragraph Essay	
Paragraph Structure	Assists Reader by
Introductory Paragraph	• Introducing topic and explaining why it is of interest • Outlining a debate about a topic • Providing a short, clear thesis statement
First Body Paragraph	• Providing a topic sentence on best point FOR thesis • Explaining the support for above statement
Second Body Paragraph	• Providing a topic sentence on second best point FOR thesis • Explaining support for above statement
Third Body Paragraph	• Providing a topic sentence on best point AGAINST thesis • Explaining support for above statement
Concluding Paragraph	• Restating thesis • Discussing why one side of debate is stronger • Finishing the essay

Once students have drafted a five-paragraph essay based on the above structure, instructors should use Appendix 12: GED Essay Grading Rubric to assess this first draft. At this stage, it is essential to remind students that essays need to go through multiple revisions. As the authors of this book will attest, revision can be frustrating but almost always improves the work. Instructors should remind students that revising is an essential and necessary part of writing a concise and clear essay. Learning to accept constructive criticism (whether students agree with it or not) is an important part of secondary and post-secondary education.

Another approach to teaching the five-paragraph essay is to use existing curricula to identify two competing positions or ways of seeing a problem or issue. This may be appropriate for GED classes—using on materials already available. For example, in social studies, civics, literature, and science, this approach might focus on debates like:

- President Abraham Lincoln was more influential than President Franklin Delano Roosevelt.

- Creationism should be taught in school alongside evolution.

- Capitalism can better protect American jobs than socialism.

Once a topic has been selected, students can work together as a class to identify arguments, evidence, and examples on either side of the debate. Instructors can group common ideas together and have the class vote on which two or three arguments are the strongest for each side. Students can make their own map of the debate using Appendix 4: Mapping Your Position. Instructors can ask questions like:

- What would those who accept one view of the debate need to argue to be convincing?

- What would those who do not accept the first view need to argue to be convincing?

Once this exercise is complete, instructors can adapt Appendix 8: The GED 5-Paragraph Essay and encourage students to draft an essay. Whatever approach is used, instructors should be sure to provide the template outlined in Appendix 9: 5-Paragraph Essays—Section-by-Section so students begin to understand what each paragraph of the essay should contain.

The final element in Step 4 is the peer review process. Once an essay has been drafted, students should be organized in pairs. Each should show his work to his partner and explain the process used to create the essay. Students read their partner's essay and make a map of the main points. Together they should go through both essays and review the Appendix 12: GED Essay Grading Rubric. Together, they should consider how well each essay matches up with each section of the rubric and write down three elements that could be improved. Each student should use the list of suggested improvements developed through the peer review to revise and/or finalize his essay.

Instructors can assist during this step by explaining that new GED requirements call for students to demonstrate critical reflection in their essays. Thus, in paragraph 3, each student should be able to provide counterevidence and explain why it challenges the thesis statement developed in the introductory paragraph. This is another good opportunity for instructors to remind students that essay writing takes practice. They can encourage students by reminding them that they will draft, revise, and redraft their essays multiple times.

As students grow more confident in their ability to write five-paragraph essays, instructors can challenge them by asking them to use their Pro/Con table to argue the position opposite from the one they presented in their initial essay. This can be challenging and invigorating for students preparing for their GED tests. As students never know what essay topic they will need to write on, this kind of practice may prove to be invaluable. Instructors should review drafted essays multiple times and provide feedback where needed. Feedback may include comments about how well student essays match the provided structure, whether the spelling is correct, and to what extent ideas are communicated effectively.

In general, we believe the use of debate principles within the GED classroom can be useful if instructors carefully review the materials they currently use. In our experience, much of the existing GED coursework can be reframed to make the most of the debate activities provided in this book. By exploring the Pros and Cons associated with various issues and topics, instructors can encourage students to read additional material and construct the best arguments for and against various propositions, including current controversies discussed on television, in newspapers, and magazines. Provided the materials are accessible for this population, debates among scholars and other experts can assist those ready to move on to more challenging coursework.

5.5 Step 5—Diagrammatic, Debate, and Dialogue (AA)

Goals for students:

- Students demonstrate an understanding of Steps 1–4 and use maps to brainstorm, organize ideas, and visually present arguments, evidence, and counterevidence

- Students can draft an 8–10 page argument essay using skills acquired though writing a number of five-paragraph essays

- Students can engage in full D³ debate, including organizing and communicating material, drafting speeches, and articulating which side of the debate they find more convincing, while acknowledging compelling counterevidence

Materials:

Appendix 5: Mapping Education and Learning Skills

Appendix 6: Barriers and Solutions Table

Appendix 14: Organizing a 5-Section Essay

Appendix 15: Principles of D^3

Appendix 16: Lesson Plan: Future of Higher Education Debate

Appendix 17: Materials: Future of Higher Education

Appendix 18: Debate and Dialogue Outline

Appendix 19: Mapping a Strategy

Appendix 20: Mapping a Speech

Appendix 21: Roles and Responsibilities

Appendix 22: Advanced Skills—Verbal

Appendix 23: Advanced Skills—Non-Verbal

Appendix 24: Assessing Debaters

The main goal of Step 5 is for students to use skills previously acquired in steps 1–4. These include transitioning from writing shorter five-paragraph essays to writing longer 8–10 page argument essays, participating in a D^3 debate, and critically reflecting on the arguments during the post-debate dialogue sessions. An essential skill is remaining respectful even during a vigorous debate.

One way to begin is to review previously acquired skills and revisit activities undertaken in Step 3. Students can make a map of their education history and reflect on their educational experience to date using Appendix 5: Mapping Education and Learning Skills. Students who completed this activity in Step 3 can compare their previous map with their current map and consider how they are the same and different. For students who have not been through steps 1–4, creating an education history (Appendix 5), identifying past barriers and solutions (Appendix 6), and a five-paragraph personal education plan (Appendix 7) can assist them in understanding past successes and challenges and their aspirations for the future. These maps may be shared with the class, while instructors can encourage students to use them to present their best and worst education experiences. These reflections can be used to suggest strategies based on past experience that can help them succeed in the AA classroom.

Another way to apply debate skills is to show students how the outline for a five-paragraph essay introduced in Step 4 can be applied to a five-section college argument essay. In Table 11, the elements of Table 10 are reproduced and repurposed to meet the expectations of the college classroom. The main difference is that each section of the argument essay should be a mini five-paragraph essay. While not each section will always contain exactly five paragraphs, by focusing on how the requirements in each section mirror the approach previously introduced, students can transition from five-paragraph GED essays to five-section college essays. Appendix 14: Organizing a 5-Section Essay provides a useful handout for students learning to develop five-section essays.

Table 11—From 5-Paragraph Essay to 5-Section Argument Essay

5-Paragraph Structure	5-Section Essay Structure	Assists Reader by
Introductory Paragraph	Introduction and Thesis Statement	• Introducing topic and explaining why it is of interest • Outlining a debate about a topic • Providing a short, clear thesis statement
First Body Paragraph —————— Second Body Paragraph	Evidence	• Providing a topic sentence on best point FOR thesis • Explaining support for above statement • Providing a topic sentence on second best point FOR thesis • Explaining support for above statement
Third Body Paragraph	Counterevidence	• Providing a topic sentence on best point AGAINST thesis • Explaining support for above statement
Concluding Paragraph	Discussion and Conclusion	• Restating thesis • Weighing and balancing arguments • Discussing why one side of debate is stronger • Concluding essay

D[3] debates can be based on specific course materials or use additional sources. They may be organized in a variety of ways. For example, we have divided the class into two equal groups and had them prepare three arguments on each side of a debate. We have also divided the class into small groups, usually of four students, and facilitated two-on-two debates based on provided materials. The most common approach has been to use debates in the place of presentations and have different students each week work in teams of two, three, or even five to present a formal debate. It is essential that D[3] be organized around three distinct activities: pre-debate planning; the debate; post-debate dialogue. The discussion below should be used alongside Appendix 15: Principles of D[3], Appendix 16: Lesson Plan: Future of Higher Education Debate, and Appendix 17: Materials: Future of Higher Education Debate.

Pre-Debate Planning

Pre-debate planning is essential. This may include group work designed to have debate teams identify the best arguments, assign speaking roles, and agree on a strategy for the debate. Instructors may pre-select teams in any way they wish. Sometimes assigning students to teams based on their known positions is useful, but more often assigning students at random to teams will ensure that at least someone on each team is required to argue against his or her own position.

As students become more comfortable, instructors can assign students to argue positions that they know the students do not hold. Instructors should do this either after they have established rapport with the class or feel confident that the individual student can handle the assignment. Instructors need to be able to explain why they have assigned that student to argue the counter position; it may be useful for instructors to refer to our previous discussion on social learning and moral development. In sum, D[3] challenges students as a part of Associate of Arts (AA) degree coursework. The ability to convincingly argue against one's own personal opinion is a way to think about the differences between ABE, GED, and AA students.

We suggest instructors frame the main proposition to be debated as a declarative statement. For example: "Juvenile offenders should never be tried as adults" or "recreational marijuana use should be decriminalized and regulated like alcohol." The way questions are framed is important. Everyone must clearly understand that the Pro team is arguing in favor of the proposition and that the Con team is arguing against the proposition. We also suggest that instructors provide in-class time for students to meet, review the D[3] outline, draft arguments, map their strategies, and prepare and practice their speeches. Materials such as Appendix 18: Debate and Dialogue Outline, Appendix 19: Mapping a Strategy, and Appendix 20: Mapping a Speech can assist students in preparing and refining their arguments. Table 12 can be useful to review the elements of the debate and assign roles to different individuals within each debate team.

Section	Roles and Responsibilities	Name(s)
Table 12—Organizing Student Debaters		
Introduction (Pro) (2–3 Mins)	• Define the topic • Present the PRO team's position • Outline briefly what the team will talk about	List name here
Introduction (Con) (2–3 Mins)	• Accept or offer alternative definition • Present the CON team's position • Outline briefly what the team will talk about	List name here
Main Body (Pro) (5–7 Mins)	• Reaffirm the PRO team's position • Provide evidence/arguments/examples that support team's position • Usually 2–3 separate points are made	List 2–3 names here
Main Body (Con) (5–7 Mins)	• Reaffirm the CON team's position • Provide evidence/arguments/examples that support team's position • Usually 2–3 separate points are made	List 2–3 names here
Questions (5–7 Mins)	• PRO asks CON 1 question • CON asks PRO 1 question • Chair selects 1–2 audience questions per team	List names here

Conclusion (Pro) (3–4 Mins)	• Restate position	List name here
	• Present a summary of case	
	• Acknowledge and answer best counterargument	
	• Conclude case for the team	
Conclusion (Con) (3–4 Mins)	• Restate position	List name here
	• Present a summary of case	
	• Acknowledge and answer best counterargument	
	• Conclude case for the team	

During the pre-debate planning phase, instructors should periodically check in with each team. These check-ins should be used to review each team's arguments, ensure that each team member is contributing more or less equally, and answer questions where needed to help clarify the main points of the debate, the proposition, or the D^3 model. Instructors should ensure that arguments are based on credible sources, organized logically, and that they flow from one to the next. Once each team has drafted a general strategy for its position, selected students should be thinking about questions to ask the other team, and possible questions the other team may ask. Encourage students to develop short, clear questions to avoid rambling statements that may address multiple points and cannot be easily answered.

Questions might try to uncover an inconsistency within the evidence or force the team to acknowledge an underlying assumption, possible negative elements of their stance, or what might happen if their position were applied in other contexts. Usually students will prepare questions based on their assumptions about the strongest argument the other team will make. This is good, but students may wish to change their question if they hear something during the course of the debate that they believe should be challenged or explored in more depth. Instructors should encourage this sort of flexibility.

Before the debate begins, instructors should ensure that both teams are prepared and review student arguments. Instructors can quiz each team separately and ask questions like:

• What is your team's position?

- What is the strongest argument?

- Will your team present it first, second, or third? Why?

- What do you expect to be the opposing team's strongest argument?

- What questions might you ask the other team?

- What questions do you expect them to ask your team?

If each team cannot answer these questions, more preparation may be needed. When both teams can answer these kinds of questions and each team has submitted an outline based on Appendix 20: Mapping a Speech, it is time to debate.

The Debate

When students are prepared and each team has turned in an outline, have the debaters bring tables and chairs to the front of the class for the formal debate. It is useful to choose someone to be the Chair or Moderator to keep the time and manage audience questions. The Chair or Moderator should create his or her own speaker's list and review it with each member of each team. The Chair should remind debaters of the order of speeches and time limits. The Chair should make sure all students have the materials they need and call the room to order and should remind the audience of the overall goals:

- Present credible information in an organized manner

- Debate different ideas that emerge from this information

- Promote respectful dialogue throughout and acknowledge counterevidence

It may also be useful to review the role and responsibilities of Debaters, Chairs, and the Audience (Table 13, also provided as Appendix 21).

Table 13—Roles and Responsibilities		
Chairs	Debaters	Audience
Collect outline documents	Prepare arguments and connect individual speeches to tell a story	Keep an open mind
Review time for speeches	Draft outline documents	Write down best arguments

Manage debate	Prepare/Predict possible questions	Prepare short, clear questions
Collect and ask audience questions	Deliver 2-minute speeches	Watch to ensure each team debates respectfully acknowledges counterarguments
Tally votes	Stay respectful at all times and answer ALL questions honestly	Vote on debate winner, respond to questions, engage in classroom dialogue

The Chair should then restate the proposition to be debated and introduce the teams. The class should be encouraged to listen carefully to each position, jot down possible questions, and think about who is making the best argument, even if they may not personally agree. In the past, we have also encouraged audience members to make a map of the arguments they hear. Appendix 4: Mapping Your Position can be a useful resource to assist audience members to visualize the main arguments presented and choose which side is closer to their own position.

Student debaters usually take their roles seriously and enjoy having the floor to deliver their speeches. In most cases, instructors can leave the facilitation to the Chair, but at times they may need to step in to remind debaters of the goals and the time constraints or to ensure that they remain respectful. The instructor and Chair may choose to modify the format. For example, it might be useful to provide an additional 30 seconds to opposing teams if they go over their allotted time or vary the number of debater and/or audience questions. Once again, as long as the debate follows the general structure outlined above and meets D³ goals, flexibility is encouraged. As students become more experienced, Appendix 22: Advanced Skills—Verbal, and Appendix 23: Advanced Skills—Non-Verbal can assist students in improving their speech, presentation, and comportment.

Post-Debate Dialogue

Following the debate, members of the audience should show their appreciation for the debaters' effort by cheering or applause. Students then vote by secret ballot to determine which side "won" the debate; writing "Pro" or "Con" on a small slip of paper should suffice. Instructors should vote if the audience is an even number. While the Chair collects the ballots and tallies the vote, instructors should debrief with the class, asking questions such as:

- What was the best argument made by each side in the debate?

- What was the best answer to a question?

- Did both sides stay respectful and acknowledge counterevidence?

- Did people vote based on their personal opinion or on how well each team presented their side of the debate?

- Would students have changed their vote if they had voted for best arguments instead of the side they personally agreed with?

It is often useful for the instructor to note two elements that each team or each speaker performed very well during the debate, and one element that could be improved. Such observations might relate to verbal or non-verbal skills, strong arguments, and good questions or answers. These can be easily compiled in a student debate assessment form like Appendix 24: Assessing Debaters.

Instructors should make sure to leave enough time (20–30 minutes) for the post-debate dialogue. Reflecting on the debate and the decision-making process by students can often be as valuable a teaching tool as the debate itself. The debrief period can be a useful time to ask debaters and the class what they might change for future debates or what they learned from that day's debate. Focusing on post-debate dialogue encourages students to express divergent viewpoints and, more important, it allows students to reflect on what they heard during the debate, why it mattered to them, and what it might mean.

6.0: DEBATE IN CORRECTIONAL SETTINGS: QUESTIONS & ANSWERS

1. How did this program evolve?

D³ emerged from work undertaken in two facilities of the Washington State Department of Corrections. It builds on the existing array of educational opportunities available to inmates, specifically the General Equivalency Diploma (GED) and the Associate of Arts (AA) degree from Walla Walla Community College (WWCC). Since 2010, our work has involved the integration of debate and dialogue into both the AA program and GED coursework, the development of a debate club for AA graduates, and the expansion of interactions and community outreach with Washington State University (WSU). More recently, D³ has been adapted by and used in a number of colleges and universities in Washington State and shared with programs around the world funded through the Open Society Foundations network.

2. Can you really debate in prisons?

In our experience, Yes! We have used debate in a variety of classes and with a variety of students. Remember that a full debate may not be possible right away. Instead, use the five-step process outlined in Section 5 to prepare your students for debate. As your students develop the skills needed to take and justify a position, begin to challenge them with higher-level activities. When students can acknowledge multiple perspectives and are ready to argue against their personal view, it is time to attempt a full debate. In our experience, debates work best when debaters commit in front of the class or assembled audience to upholding the values and principles of D³ and stay respectful throughout the debate.

3. What is the benefit of using debate in my classroom?

Using debate has a number of benefits, as outlined in Section 3.4. Perhaps the most interesting and valuable result is how debate can spur students to take a more active role in their own education. By encouraging them to stake out and justify different positions on issues, instructors can spur cognitive development. By having to find credible sources to support positions, students are encouraged to think critically about the way in which knowledge is constructed and presented. Finally, by modeling pro-social interactions and respectful dialogue, debate helps us demonstrate to one another that disagreements need not become disagreeable, angry, or physical.

4. Are all topics debatable?

A very good question. In general, we would say yes. Of course, both sides must be based on arguments drawn from credible sources. Provided disagreement exists between or among respected scholars or experts, most topics can be debated. We have debated contentious subjects like abortion, climate change, punishment and/ or rehabilitation in the criminal justice system, and same-sex marriage. However, these more complicated topics are perhaps best left to more advanced students and classes. In the short-to-medium term, debates can be built on existing coursework. This allows students to develop debate-related skills, while working in areas in which they will later be tested. We encourage instructors in college-level classes to keep an open mind when determining a topic. Offer students choices and spend some time finding good sources for them to use in their research. These sources will lead to more refined arguments, but neither students nor instructors need to agree with all arguments presented. As long as the arguments are based on credible sources and made respectfully, promoting dialogue on topics of interest can be extremely useful in the classroom and beyond.

5. What happens if debates devolve into arguments among students?

Argument is an acceptable part of debate. However, disrespect is not. It is essential that instructors share the guiding principles of D³ with their students. One of the guiding principles is: Debates ALWAYS employ respectful discourse and disagreement. Personal attacks or insults undermine the value and importance of debates and will not be tolerated. However, there is a difference between debates in which debaters passionately make their case and the devolution of an argument into the sort of heated back-and-forth characteristic of some cable news stations. Some students with debate experience or those who are heavy consumers of popular media may revert to that behavior. Instructors must discourage it. One approach is to have the debaters commit to the values and principles that underlie the model. If the debate becomes heated, issue a warning. If the students cannot abide by the principles of the D³ model, the debate should be immediately called off. Instructors should carefully explain why it was cancelled. Ask for suggestions about how the class can attempt another debate in the future.

6. How have debate activities been used to promote community engagement?

Debate activities have been used in a variety of ways throughout the United States and beyond. For example, in 2012, Walla Walla Community College (WWCC) at Coyote Ridge Corrections Center and Washington State University (WSU) held debate events in which mixed teams of students from WSU and WWCC graduates from the AA degree program worked together. The WSU students were juniors and seniors in good standing in the Department of Criminal Justice and Criminology. The WWCC students had earned their degrees while incarcerated and were part of the debate club. Students met three times over the semester to: 1) brainstorm the benefits and challenges of debate and to pick a debate topic; 2) work together to organize the best arguments and decide who would play what role within the debate; and 3) participate in a five-on-five mixed team debate at the prison for other incarcerated students, WSU students, Department of Corrections staff, and interested community members. In partnership with the Center for Civic Engagement at WSU, these events explored the role of debate in presenting information, exploring different perspectives, and promoting dialogue between and among the debaters and the audience.

7. Where can I get more information about debate?

<u>General Resources</u>

International Debate Education Association
www.idebate.org

Walla Walla High School Debate Team Resources
https://sites.google.com/site/wahispeechanddebateclub/handouts

Washington Debate Coalition
http://www.washingtondebate.org/

<u>Debate Topics and Links for Resources Appropriate for GED Debates</u>

Lesson Plans and More Resources for Classroom Debates
http://www.educationworld.com/a_lesson/lesson/lesson304b.shtml

Middle School Debate Resources
http://www.middleschooldebate.com/topics/topicresearch.htm

<u>Debate Topics and Links for AA Instructors</u>

The Economist Debates
http://www.economist.com/debate/archive

National Forensic League
http://www.nflonline.org/StudentResources/Topics

CONCLUSION

This book has sought to identify the goals and core principles of D^3, consider the role of educational programming in correctional settings, and provide the philosophic and pedagogic basis for the use of debate. Of specific importance has been the desire to offer some practical steps to use debates in AA and GED classrooms and the provision of different key resources and examples that can be used by instructors and students.

Classroom debates are not appropriate for all classrooms or students. However, their value historically has been connected to the variety of functional, critical, and interactional skills they promote. Debate fosters research ability, organization, and communication skills. It also promotes critical thinking skills associated with evaluating arguments and their construction, along with fostering judgment about how positions and evidence are connected. Perhaps of most utility is the inherent flexibility of classroom debates to meet the needs of different instructors and classrooms.

Based on our experience, the process of debate offers profound and lasting benefits for individuals in correctional settings. By emphasizing critical thinking, effective communication, independent research, and teamwork, debate teaches skills that assist individuals in fulfilling their responsibilities as citizens of democratic societies. Perhaps of most importance is how debate can encourage us to confront our own biases and attempt to understand other perspectives.

While this book has focused on how D^3 can be applied in correctional settings, we believe there is no limit to where this model of debate can be used. From classrooms to community centers, the value of this approach lies in its ability to promote engagement and respectful discourse. This approach values both the effort of developing and presenting a position on a contentious topic, as well as the participation of those gathered to listen, learn, question, and consider. We hope to hear from you about your experiences integrating debate into your teaching in correctional settings or elsewhere. What worked? What didn't? How have you adapted the material presented in this book? Drop us a line via Johannes Wheeldon at (jwheeldon@gmail.com).

Appendixes:
Resources For Instructors

No.	Step	Description
1	1	Making a Map
1a	1	Introductory Map
1b	1	Blank Map Template A
1c	1	Blank Map Template B
1d	1	Blank Map Template C
2	1 & 2	Pro/Con Map
3	2	Pro/Con Table
4	2	Mapping Your Position
5	3	Mapping Education and Learning Skills
6	3	Barriers and Solutions Table
7	3	5-Paragraph Personal Education Plan
8	3	The GED 5-Paragraph Essay
9	3 & 4	5-Paragraph Essays—Section-by-Section
10	4	Exploring Essay Topics Using Pro/Con Tables
11	4	Drafting Essays Using Maps

12	4	GED Essay Grading Rubric
13	4 & 5	Mapping an AA debate
14	5	Organizing a 5-Section Essay
15	5	Principles of D^3
16	5	Lesson Plan: Future of Higher Education Debate
17	5	Materials: Future of Higher Education Debate
18	5	Debate and Dialogue Model Outline
19	5	Mapping a Debate Strategy
20	5	Mapping a Speech
21	5	Roles and Responsibilities
22	5	Advanced Skills—Verbal
23	5	Advanced Skills—Non-Verbal
24	5	Assessing Debaters

APPENDIX 1: MAKING A MAP

One way to make a map is by brainstorming. Try to visually connect your ideas. You can make a visual idea map in five easy steps.

	Making Visual Maps in Five Steps	
Step	Description	
1	Make a list of six to eight (6–8) concepts related to a topic of interest	
2	Starting in the middle of the page, write the name of the topic and draw two lines outward (one to the left and one to the right)	
3	At the end of the lines, use two concepts to show two different perspectives on the topic	
4	Now connect the remaining concepts from your list to the two perspectives to show how each is or is not related	
5	Review your map and show it to another student or the instructor. Does he understand what your map represents?	

Here is a diagram about making a map based on the table above.

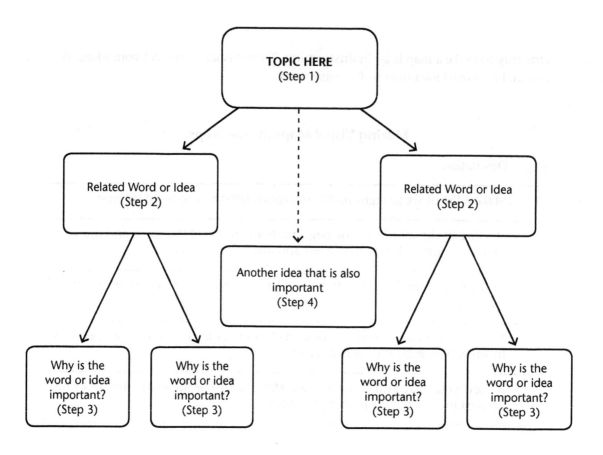

Appendixes 1a–1d provide three other templates you can use and adapt as needed.

1a. Introductory Map

Title/Topic_____

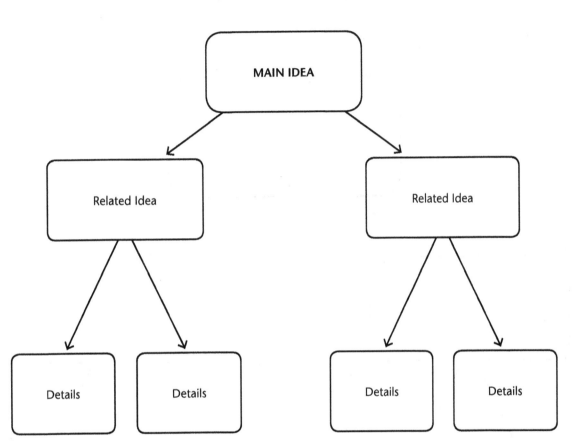

1b. Blank Map Template A

You can use this map to get comfortable with the mapping process. Start with a key word in the top box and include related terms below

Title/Topic_____

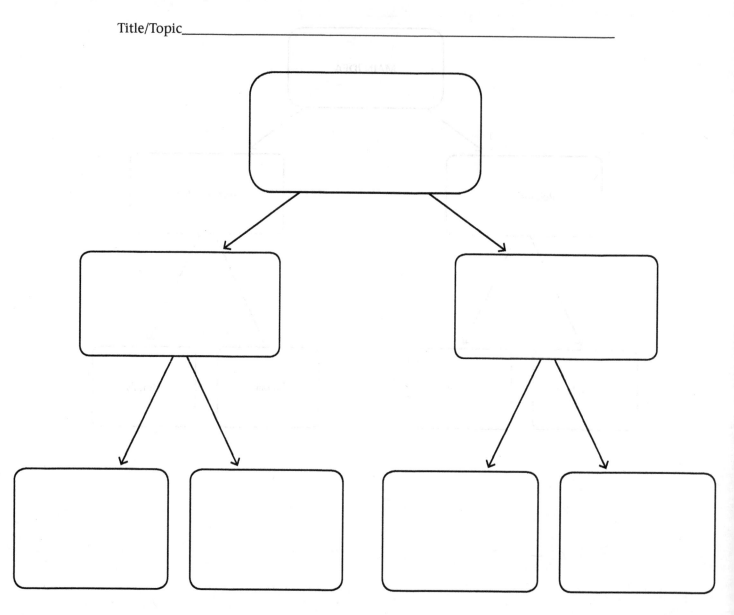

Debate and Dialogue in Correctional Settings

1c. Blank Map Template B

You can use this map to get comfortable with the mapping process. Start with a key word in the bottom box and include related terms above.

Title/Topic_____

1d. Blank Map Template C

You can use this map to get comfortable with the mapping process. Start with a key word in the middle circle. Next, think of related terms that could go around the middle circle. Finally, provide examples of each related term in the boxes in the corners.

Title/Topic_____

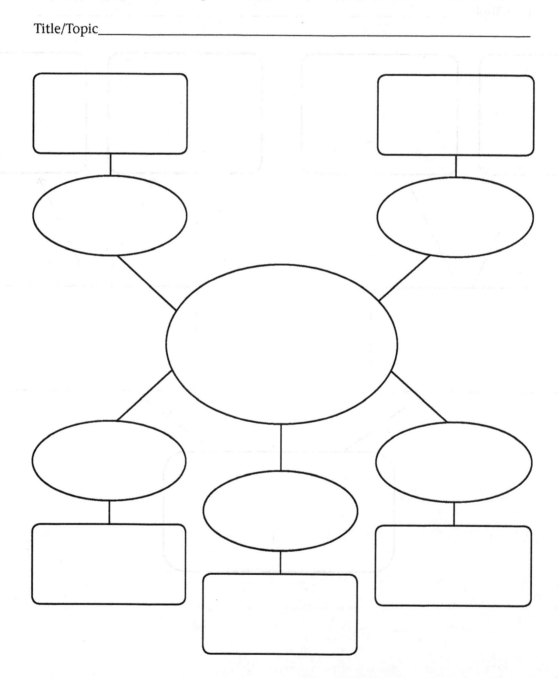

APPENDIX 2: PRO/CON MAP

When you are analyzing a topic, you can use a pro/con map to outline both sides of the issue. Try to think of two arguments for and against a topic. Add more arrows and boxes if you think of additional arguments.

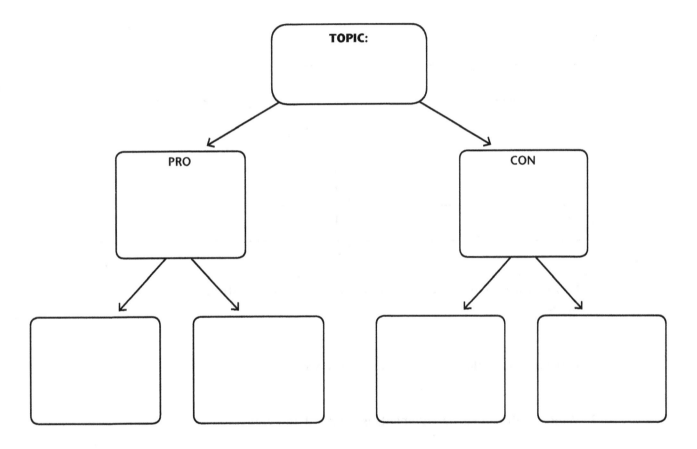

APPENDIX 3: PRO/CON TABLE

Based on the topic, identify Pros and Cons. One strategy is to provide the opposite of each example you list. Try to put your strongest arguments first on each side of the table based on the numbers below.

Topic:

PRO	CON
1.	1.
2.	2.
3.	3.
4.	4.
5.	5.

1. Please explain why you think the top two arguments are stronger than the others.

2. Explain which side you would choose and why.

3. Which of the opposing arguments is strongest and why?

Additional Notes and Comments:

APPENDIX 4: MAPPING YOUR POSITION

Using your Pro/Con table, map your position. You may use the format below, or make your own. Rank the arguments from strongest (box 1) to weakest (box 3).

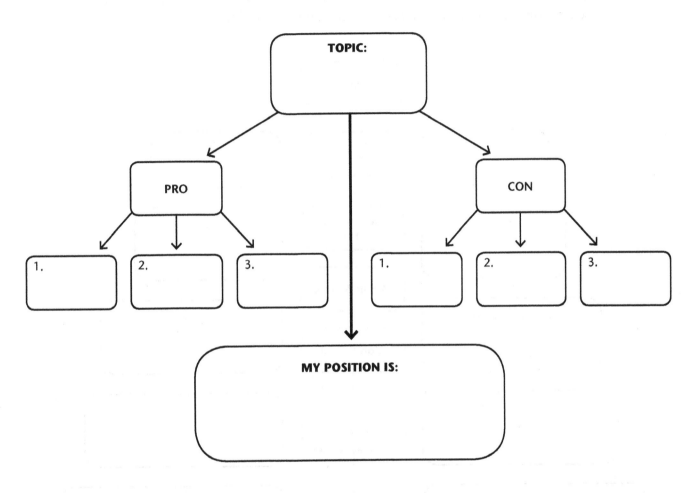

APPENDIX 5: MAPPING EDUCATION AND LEARNING SKILLS

Using the template below, make your own map of your education and learning skills, focusing on your past educational experience and goals for the future.

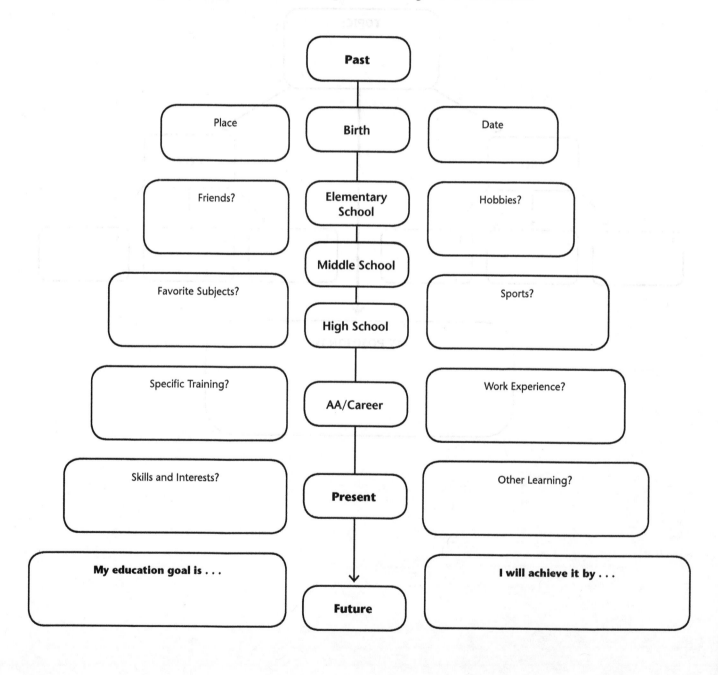

APPENDIX 6: BARRIERS AND SOLUTIONS TABLE

Use this table to focus on ways to overcome past education barriers based on the map you made in Appendix 5. It may be useful to use headings for each box as provided below. When you have completed the Barriers and Solutions columns, consider what conclusions you might draw from your map and this table.

Identifying Barriers and Solutions Based on Educational History	
Barrier	Solution

Conclusions

APPENDIX 7: 5-PARAGRAPH PERSONAL EDUCATION PLAN

Using the example below, create your own Personal Education Plan. You should use the materials you developed in Appendix 5 and Appendix 6.

Paragraph Structure	Contains	My Personal Education Plan
Introductory Paragraph	• Statement about why education is important • A past education challenge • A personal education goal	•
First Body Paragraph	• Outline of one strategy to attain goal • Examples or related ideas	•
Second Body Paragraph	• Outline of another strategy to attain goal • Examples or related ideas	•
Third Body Paragraph	• Biggest past education barrier/challenge • Possible strategy to circumvent this barrier	•
Concluding Paragraph	• Restatement of personal education goal • Discussion of strategies to attain goal and overcome barriers	•

APPENDIX 8: THE GED 5-PARAGRAPH ESSAY

This lesson plan can be used in all GED classes but is most appropriate for students who have acquired the skills associated with brainstorming, organizing, and drafting a 5-Paragraph Education Plan.

Instructors can use any existing resources that provide essay topic examples or use the topics provided in Appendixes 10 and 11.

Previously Acquired Skills and Activities:

Appendix 5: Mapping Education and Learning Skills

Appendix 6: Barrier and Solutions Table

Appendix 7: 5-Paragraph Personal Education Plan

Materials:

Appendix 1: Making a Map

Appendix 2: Pro/Con Map

Appendix 3: Pro/Con Table

Appendix 4: Mapping Your Position

Appendix 8: The GED 5-Paragraph Essay

Appendix 9: 5-Paragraph Essay—Section-by-Section

Appendix 10: Exploring Essay Topics Using Pro/Con Tables

Appendix 11: Drafting Essay Topics Using Maps

Appendix 12: GED Essay Rubric

Purpose and Objective(s):

- Students will use the structure and reasoning behind a Pro/Con argument to construct a five-paragraph GED argumentative essay

- Students will be introduced to the concept through a sample GED essay topic "The positive and negative effects of television"

- Students will work in groups to come up with examples of Pro and Con arguments and use the Idea Map to brainstorm and the Pro/Con Table to organize their ideas

- Students will draft a five-paragraph argumentative essay based on the provided format that demonstrates that they can understand issues from both sides and choose their side based on the arguments most compelling to them

Introduction:

This lesson introduces students to organizing their ideas into pro con/compare and contrast viewpoints specifically required for GED essays. The instructor should lead the discussion on the topic "Television has a positive influence on its viewers." He or she will:

- Show students how to structure their responses to the prompt in a Pro/Yes or Con/No manner for an idea map on the board (Appendix 1)

- Give students copies of Pro/Con Maps (Appendix 2) and Pro/Con sheets (Appendix 3). Make additional copies of the maps or Pro/Con sheet as needed

- Ask students to present their opinions on the positives and negatives of television to the class. This can be done as a whole class or in large or small groups

- Ask students to choose their side of the argument and begin a pro or con idea map. They must also recognize the best counterargument of the opposing side using the Pro/Con table in Appendix 3.

Drafting & Feedback:

Students should be given time to work on their idea map, Pro and Con arguments, and essay structure alone and then in small groups. The instructor should facilitate student discussion and answer questions. Students should be open to other students' examples and actively listen to the details of the arguments both for and against.

The instructor will provide the Pro/Con map (Appendix 2), Pro/Con table (Appendix 3), and Mapping Your Position (Appendix 4). Once students complete the tables and maps, instructors can provide Appendix 9: 5-Paragraph Essays—Section-by-Section.

Assessing Student Learning & Next Steps:

The standardized GED Essay scoring guide should be used to grade students (Appendix 12: GED Essay Grading Rubric). Once students have completed their essay on television viewing, the instructor will review them and offer feedback.

Advanced students can review the essay examples provided in Appendixes 10 and 11 and begin to construct additional argumentative essays, making sure to follow the organizational structure of a 5-paragraph GED essay (Appendix 9). Encourage students to create their own idea map and or pro/con form (Appendix 1, 2, or 3).

APPENDIX 9: 5-PARAGRAPH ESSAY— SECTION-BY-SECTION

The five-paragraph essay is a useful way to summarize two views on a topic or issue and demonstrate the opinion of the essay's author about which view is stronger and why.

Paragraph Structure	Assists Reader by
Introductory Paragraph	• Introducing topic and explaining why it is of interest • Outlining a debate about a topic • Providing a short, clear thesis statement
First Body Paragraph	• Providing a topic sentence on best point FOR thesis • Explaining the support for above statement
Second Body Paragraph	• Providing a topic sentence on second best point FOR thesis • Explaining support for above statement
Third Body Paragraph	• Providing a topic sentence on best point AGAINST thesis • Explaining support for above statement
Concluding Paragraph	• Restating thesis • Discussing why one side of debate is stronger • Concluding essay

APPENDIX 10: EXPLORING ESSAY TOPICS USING PRO/CON TABLES

Section 1: Please pick a topic statement and complete the Pro/Con Table. Once you have at least two arguments for Pro and two arguments for Con, use these to answer the questions below.

Pro/Con Table	
Topic:	
PRO	CON
1.	1.
2.	2.
3.	3.
4.	4.
5.	5.

1. In your opinion which side of the argument is stronger? Why?

2. Using the Pro/Con Table, please list the two best arguments for the side of the argument that you agree with.

3. In your opinion which is the best counterargument?

Additional Notes and Comments:

Section 2. Answer the following questions using the tables provided.

1. If you could live in a small town or a big city which would you choose? What are some of the positives and negatives of your choice? For example, if you chose to live in a small town, a positive would be less crime, but a negative would be not a lot to do. In a big city, a negative would be more traffic, but a positive would be more job opportunities. Pick whether you think you could live in a small town or big city. Then list the positives and negatives of your choice.

I Would Live in a:	
Positives	Negatives

2. Who do you think was a better U.S. president, George W. Bush or Bill Clinton? In your essay, mention your political party affiliation and consider Pro/Con arguments for each president below. For example, you might mention that you support the Republican Party. You could argue that while economic growth occurred under President Bill Clinton, he was impeached. In this example, you might argue that President George W. Bush did a good job implementing the No Child Left Behind Act to make schools more accountable, but took the United States into an unpopular war in Iraq.

President Bush		President Clinton	
PRO	CON	PRO	CON

3. Do you agree or disagree with the idea that creationism should be taught along-side evolution in U.S. schools? In your essay, describe three specific points that support your opinion, but also mention one opposing point that you think has some validity.

Agree	Disagree

APPENDIX 11: DRAFTING ESSAYS USING MAPS

For some students, mapping out their topic can be more effective. Using the instructions in Appendix 1, read through the GED materials and make a map that includes arguments for and against the propositions below. Your map should be based on the information provided in your GED textbook and/or other related materials. Your map can be used to make a table; then turn your table into a five-paragraph essay.

Topic 1—Good Parents

Write an essay that describes the characteristics of a good parent.

Topic 2—Diverse Backgrounds

Write an essay that explains why people of diverse backgrounds need to get along better than they do today.

Topic 3—Defining Success

Write an essay that considers two ways to define success. Say which definition you favor and explain why.

Topic 4—Assessing Lincoln and FDR

Write an essay that argues that Arbraham Lincoln was more influential as U.S. president than Franklin Delano Roosevelt.

Topic 5—Arguing Against Yourself

Do you think socialism or capitalism is a better economic system for workers?

If you think that socialism is better, write an essay that maintains that capitalism is better than socialism for most workers.

If you think that capitalism is better, write an essay that maintains that socialism is better than capitalism for most workers.

APPENDIX 12: GED ESSAY GRADING RUBRIC

The rubric below is based on past GED standards and the new GED 2014 requirements. By including critical reflection in GED essays, students demonstrate their level of college readiness.

Graded Elements	1 Inadequate	2 Marginal	3 Adequate	4 Effective
Overall Effectiveness of the Essay	Often difficult for reader to follow writer's ideas	At times difficult for reader to follow writer's ideas	Reader can follow essay and often understands writer's ideas	Reader can follow essay and fully understand writer's ideas
Addresses Topic/Question	Doesn't address topic	Addresses topic but focus wanders	Addresses topic but does not list main points	Clearly addresses topic and lists main points
Organization	Essay is unorganized, with little focus on structure	Some evidence of organization and structure	Structure is used to make writing more effective	Structure is well organized and effectively conveys ideas
Development and Details	Little development of ideas or details, few examples	Some development in essay but few specific details	Some development in essay; examples and details given	Compelling and creative discussion of ideas, details, and examples
Compare and Contrast	No clear evidence or counterevidence provided	Some evidence but no counter-evidence provided	Clear evidence and some counter-evidence provided	Clear evidence and counter-evidence provided

Language and Spelling	Problems with writing conventions throughout	Inconsistent use of writing conventions	Consistent use of writing conventions	Generally error-free use of writing conventions
Word Choice	Includes weak or inappropriate terms or words	Demonstrates narrow range of word choice or terms	Use of varied words and terms chosen for effect	Exhibits varied word choice and precise use of terms

APPENDIX 13: MAPPING AN AA DEBATE

You may use the template below to map one or both sides of a debate.

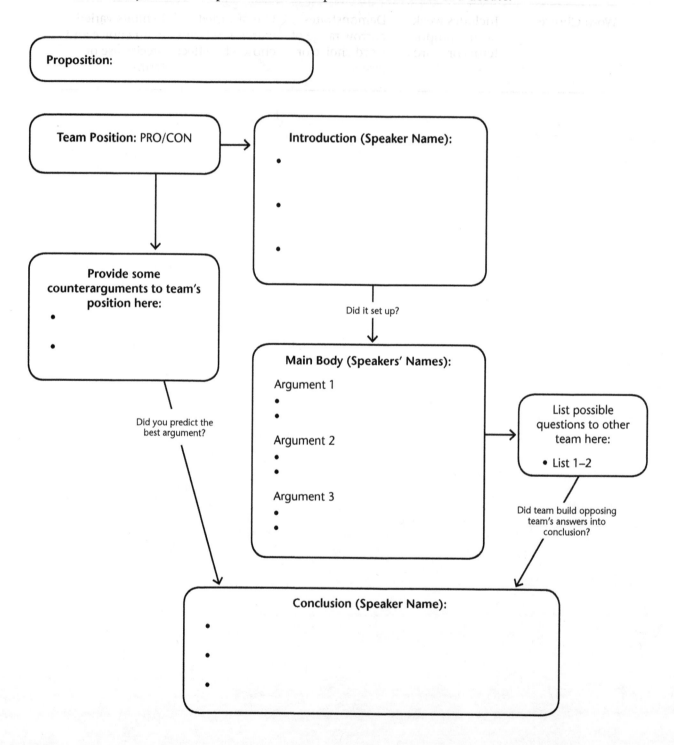

Proposition:

Team Position: PRO/CON

Introduction (Speaker Name):

-
-
-

Provide some counterarguments to team's position here:

-
-

Did it set up?

Did you predict the best argument?

Main Body (Speakers' Names):

Argument 1
-
-

Argument 2
-
-

Argument 3
-
-

List possible questions to other team here:

- List 1–2

Did team build opposing team's answers into conclusion?

Conclusion (Speaker Name):

-
-
-

APPENDIX 14: ORGANIZING A 5-SECTION ESSAY

This grid for a five-section essay provides section headings and the requirements for each.

5-Section Essay Structure	Assists Reader by
Introduction and Thesis Statement	• Introducing topic and explaining why it is of interest • Outlining a debate about a topic • Providing a short, clear thesis statement
Evidence	• Providing a topic sentence on best point • FOR thesis • Explaining the support for above statement • Providing a topic sentence on second best point FOR thesis • Explaining support for above statement • Providing a topic sentence on third best point FOR thesis • Explaining support for above statement
Counterevidence	• Providing a topic sentence on best point AGAINST thesis • Providing a topic sentence on second best point AGAINST thesis • Explaining support for above statement

Discussion	• Weighing and balancing arguments
	• Discussing why one side of debate is stronger
	• Including personal experience/bias considerations
Conclusion	• Restating thesis
	• Summarizing best arguments
	• Concluding the essay

APPENDIX 15: PRINCIPLES OF D³

D³ seeks to foster reason, tolerance, and understanding and to model pro-social interactions. The explicit assumption underlying the model is that people of good conscience may reasonably and respectfully disagree on issues of public concern. The model is based on five core principles.

1. **Debate can be used to serve a variety of educational goals.** Debates are based on research, organization, and presentation but can be employed to meet various learning needs and goals. Students should be given time in class to prepare and draft debate outline documents and/or diagrams for instructors to review and approve.

2. **Debates should be informational opportunities.** Students review arguments and use visual maps and diagrams to logically connect related ideas based on credible sources and to then construct an argument that addresses the debate topic.

3. **Debates should be conducted in ways that value the skill of presenting a coherent argument.** Success is not based solely on which team wins, but on how well teams present evidence and examples that support their position.

4. **Debates ALWAYS employ respectful discourse and disagreement.** Personal attacks or insults undermine the value and importance of debates and will not be tolerated.

5. **Debaters interact courteously and answer questions honestly.** Debaters must answer audience, instructor, or opposing team questions civilly and acknowledge the best counterarguments before offering concluding remarks.

APPENDIX 16: LESSON PLAN: FUTURE OF HIGHER EDUCATION DEBATE

This is a lesson plan for use by instructors to introduce debate into the classroom.

Outcomes:

- Students will explore debate and dialogue. They will become familiar with what debate is and why it is used in the educational process.

- Students will identify and organize arguments, evidence, and examples based on provided material.

- Students can articulate well which side of the debate they found more convincing and identify their own bias on an issue.

Materials:

Appendix 17: Materials: Future of Higher Education

Appendix 18: Debate and Dialogue Outline

Appendix 19: Mapping a Strategy

Appendix 20: Mapping a Speech

Appendix 22: Advanced Skills—Verbal

Appendix 23: Advanced Skills—Non-Verbal

Appendix 24: Assessing Debaters

Lessons:

These four lessons have been developed to work as stand-alone activities in concurrent classes or can be combined as needed. These lessons should be used in conjunction with Step 5 in Section 5.5.

Generally, students need a class to be able to: read, identify arguments, and work together to discuss the strongest arguments on each side of the debate (Lessons 1 and 2). An additional class may be used to select teams, develop speeches, and map each team's argument (Lesson 3) before engaging on the debate and dialogue (Lesson 4).

Lesson 1

Students are assigned the reading (Appendix 17: Materials: Future of Higher Education) and will be asked to identify the main argument of each piece individually and of the two examples of evidence provided by the author.

Lesson 2

Instructors facilitate a class discussion to outline two opposing arguments and related examples. If possible, students put the results of this brainstorming session on the board if possible;

Lesson 3

Instructors assign Pro/Con teams. Team members work together to identify the three best arguments and decide: a) who will introduce their presentation; b) who will make 2–3 arguments in favor of the team's position; and c) who will ask and answer questions.

Maps and diagrams should be used to organize debate outlines and summarize each speech. Students should review key verbal and non-verbal debate skills and other resources provided in Appendixes 18–23.

Instructors should also select Chairs and meet with them to review the debate outline and develop questions that they could ask each team if audience participation is minimal. Chairs should work with non-debating students to decide the proposition to be debated. For example: should it be "A college education should focus on career certificates" or "A college education should focus on teamwork and critical thinking skills"?

All students should review the reading and the debate outline. They should be prepared to explain key aspects of the introduction, main body, and conclusion. Non-debating students should be encouraged to write a question they would like answered and/or review key verbal and non-verbal debate skills and other resources provided below.

Lesson 4

When everyone is ready, hold the debate. Follow the instructions provided in the instructor roles in section 4.3 of the main text. Once everyone is in place, the instructor should review the roles and responsibilities chart (Appendix 21). Debaters must agree to debate based on the values and principles of the program as listed Appendix 15. Do NOT ignore the need to follow the D^3 format provided and debrief with the class following the debate. As the ballots are being collected and tallied, instructors should debrief with the class. They may ask general questions such as:

- What was the best argument made by each side in the debate?

- What was the best answer to a question?

- Did people vote based on their personal opinion or on how well each team presented their side of the debate?

- Would students have changed their vote if they had voted for best arguments instead of the side they personally agreed with?

APPENDIX 17: MATERIALS: FUTURE OF HIGHER EDUCATION DEBATE

1. In a Tough Economy, New Focus on Job-Oriented Certificates
Source: Adapted from Joanne Jacobs, The Hechinger Report, (Jan. 18, 2011) http://hechingerreport.org

Labor economists and some educators believe career-driven degrees should become increasingly common and are advising students to pursue skills-oriented fields of study that offer better job opportunities. Fueling the trend is the worst economic decline in more than 70 years and a slowly falling unemployment rate of 9.4 percent. Add to that the staggering total of $830 billion in student debt nationally. "The recession has brought in clear focus the value of a career versus a job," said Willis Holcombe, chancellor of Florida's fast-growing community college system. A new report based on the state's employment data shows that students who earn certificates or associate of science degrees make more money in their first year out of college than four-year graduates of Florida's university system. The unemployment numbers are "a powerful case for completing a credential," Holcombe said. "If you want to insulate yourself against unemployment, you need a career."

Nationally, 27 percent of people with licenses and certificates also earn more than the average person with a bachelor's degree, according to Anthony Carnevale, director of the Georgetown University Center on Education and the Workforce. Carnevale's newest data show that at least half of all anticipated job opportunities in the next seven years will be open to "middle-skill" workers like pharmacy technicians—what Omid Khorasani will be after he passes a certification exam. Training for such jobs is offered at both community colleges and at for-profit career and trade schools.

Middle-skills jobs require more than a high school diploma but less than a college degree, along with significant education and training—and they make up roughly half of all U.S. jobs, according to the Urban Institute, a nonprofit policy research organization based in Washington, D.C. Nursing, medical technology, and other health care jobs are growing rapidly, according to the Bureau of Labor Statistics. Even in Michigan, where the unemployment rate is 12.4 percent—tied with California for the second-highest nationally—those with associate degrees in nursing and allied health fields can find jobs, said James Jacobs, president of Macomb Community College in Warren.

Advanced manufacturing and engineering technicians with a certificate or associate of applied science degree are in demand, too, said Julian Alssid of the Workforce Strategy Center. Middle-skill workers are finding jobs in high-tech manufacturing, construction, and the energy industry, says Rachel Unruh of the National Skills Coalition, based in Washington, D.C.Many community college students are finding that their degrees are in high demand. In Pittsburg, California, students who complete a two-year associate of science degree in the Power Pathways program can qualify for a job as an apprentice electrician at Pacific Gas & Electric, starting at $64,418 per year. Recruiters descended upon the class that graduated on December 20, said Katie Romans, a spokesperson for PG&E.

2. What You Don't Know About Liberal Arts Colleges
Source: Adapted from Lynn O'Shaughnessy, CBS Money Watch, (January 21, 2010)
http://www.cbsnews.com/8301-505145_162-37241390/5-reasons-to-attend-a-liberal-arts-college/

Are 4-year liberal arts degrees a luxury and is career education the only way to go? No one could be against equipping oneself for a career. But the career education bandwagon seems to suggest that shortcuts are available to students that lead directly to high-paying jobs—leaving out so-called frills like learning how to write and speak well, how to understand the nuances of literary texts and scientific concepts, how to collaborate with others on research.

Liberal arts colleges aren't just about "frills." A liberal arts education includes the sciences and math and the national unemployment rate for four-year college graduates is under 5%, compared with more than 13% for young people with only a high school diploma. President Barack Obama wants the United States to lead the world in college degrees by 2020, with all Americans completing at least one year of post-secondary education—which is seen as the dividing line between living in poverty and a shot at a middle-class lifestyle.

Perhaps the most important fact to recognize is that employers value liberal arts. One of the missions of liberal arts colleges is to teach kids how to think, talk, and write. A survey by the Association of American Colleges and Universities released a study in 2009 that found that 89% of surveyed employers said they want college students to pursue a liberal arts education. According to the National Association of Colleges and Employers, this is because workplace success requires the ability to utilize three core skills that a liberal arts education can impart: communication skills, analytic skills, and teamwork skills.

Of course, not everyone is ready for the expectations of a traditional 4-year liberal arts college right out of high school, and many assume that without an Ivy League degree, college costs too much and provides too little in return. The bottom line is that we should still be encouraging students who are ready to attend college and provide other options for those without the financial support, grades, or determination to complete it. However we should stop questioning the value of college if it encourages students to make more thoughtful, informed decisions and allows them to be exposed to new ideas and high standards.

Plenty of evidence suggests that, on average, a college degree is worth it. The University of Washington reports that college graduates, on average, earn twice as much as non-college grads and more than a million dollars more over their lifetime than those with 2-year degrees. A 2011 report by the Brookings Institution suggested that the return on a college investment is more than that on almost any alternative, including stocks, bonds, gold, or the housing market.

While a 4-year college may not be practical for everyone, the skills acquired through a liberal arts education are neither "liberal" nor based around "arts." Without critical thinking skills, we may be trading career degrees for the more complex abilities required to meaningfully engage as citizens.

APPENDIX 18: DEBATE AND DIALOGUE MODEL OUTLINE

Section	Roles and Responsibilities
Introduction (Pro) (2–3 Mins)	• Define the topic • Present the PRO team's position • Outline briefly what the team will talk about
Introduction (Con) (2–3 Mins)	• Accept or offer alternative definition • Present the CON team's position • Outline briefly what the team will present
Main Body (Pro) (5–7 Mins)	• Reaffirm the PRO team's position • Provide evidence/arguments/examples that support team's position • Usually 2–3 separate points are made here
Main Body (Con) (5–7 Mins)	• Reaffirm the CON team's position • Provide evidence/arguments/examples that support team's position • Usually 2–3 separate points are made here
Questions (5–7 Mins)	• PRO asks CON 1 question • CON asks PRO 1 question • Chair selects 1–2 audience questions per team

Conclusion (Pro) (3–4 Mins)	• Restate position
	• Present a summary of case
	• Acknowledge and answer best counterargument
	• Conclude case for their team
Conclusion (Con) (3–4 Mins)	• Restate position
	• Present a summary of case
	• Acknowledge and answer best counterargument
	• Conclude case for their team

APPENDIX 19: MAPPING A DEBATE STRATEGY

Use the template below to make your own map of a team argument. Make sure to answer each point listed.

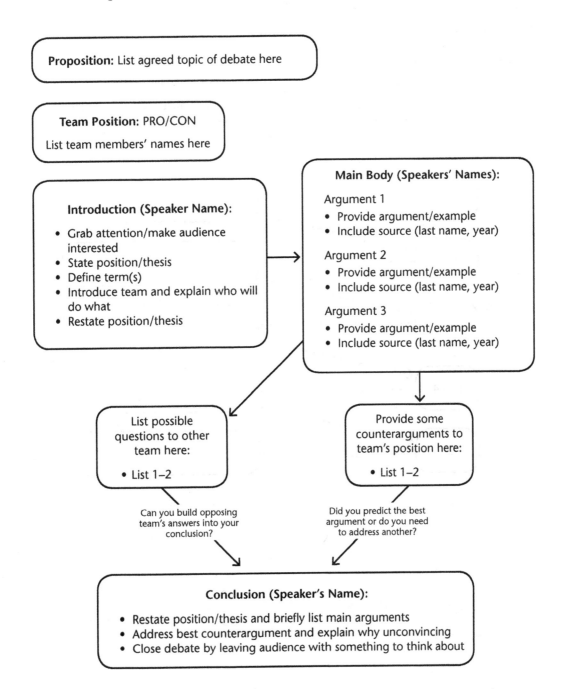

Proposition: List agreed topic of debate here

Team Position: PRO/CON

List team members' names here

Introduction (Speaker Name):

- Grab attention/make audience interested
- State position/thesis
- Define term(s)
- Introduce team and explain who will do what
- Restate position/thesis

Main Body (Speakers' Names):

Argument 1
- Provide argument/example
- Include source (last name, year)

Argument 2
- Provide argument/example
- Include source (last name, year)

Argument 3
- Provide argument/example
- Include source (last name, year)

List possible questions to other team here:

- List 1–2

Provide some counterarguments to team's position here:

- List 1–2

Can you build opposing team's answers into your conclusion?

Did you predict the best argument or do you need to address another?

Conclusion (Speaker's Name):

- Restate position/thesis and briefly list main arguments
- Address best counterargument and explain why unconvincing
- Close debate by leaving audience with something to think about

APPENDIX 20: MAPPING A SPEECH

Use this to map out your two-minute speech.

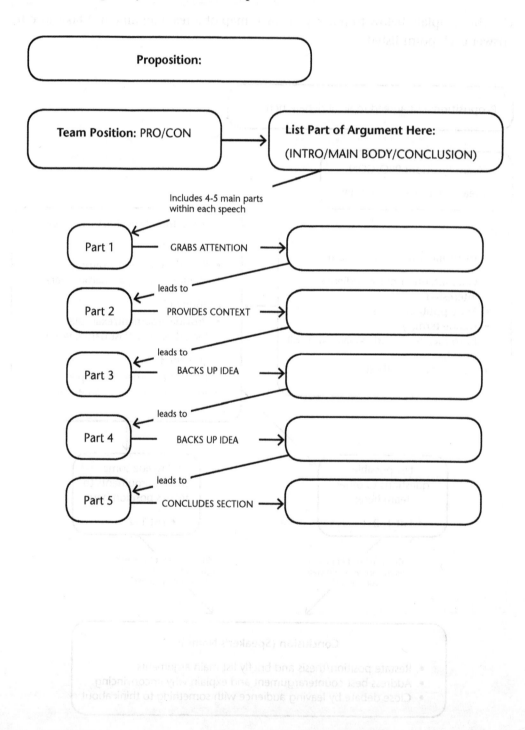

| | Proposition: | |

| | | |
| Team Position: PRO/CON | → | List Part of Argument Here:
(INTRO/MAIN BODY/CONCLUSION) |

Includes 4-5 main parts
within each speech

| Part 1 | GRABS ATTENTION → | |

leads to

| Part 2 | PROVIDES CONTEXT → | |

leads to

| Part 3 | BACKS UP IDEA → | |

leads to

| Part 4 | BACKS UP IDEA → | |

leads to

| Part 5 | CONCLUDES SECTION → | |

APPENDIX 21: ROLES AND RESPONSIBILITIES

This table can be used to introduce or remind debate participants of their various roles and responsibilities.

Chairs	Debaters	Audience
Collect outline documents	Prepare arguments and connect individual speeches to tell a story	Keep an open mind
Review time for speeches	Draft outline documents	Write down best arguments
Manage debate	Prepare/Predict possible questions	Prepare short, clear questions
Collect and ask audience questions	Deliver 2-minute speeches	Watch to ensure each team debates respectfully and acknowledges counterarguments
Tally votes	Stay respectful at all times and answer ALL questions honestly	Vote on debate winner, respond to questions, engage in classroom dialogue

APPENDIX 22: ADVANCED SKILLS—VERBAL

Verbal Skills	Description
Clarity	Effective communication depends almost exclusively on your clarity. Start by making sure you understand what you want to say. Limit the jargon and technical language and use concise statements—short and to the point—whenever you can.
Volume	You want to sound energetic and enthusiastic, but not too loud. You also may want to slightly raise your voice at times for emphasis.
Pitch	Vary your tone and avoid a repetitive inflection of rising or falling as your sentence goes on. Don't use a fake "debate voice" or inflection. Be yourself and be conversational in pitch and project from your stomach, not your throat or nose. Relaxing will help your pitch.
Rate	Most debaters go too fast for their own clarity and garble their words. Speed without clarity is harmful to your ability to persuade your audience. Most debaters would actually effectively communicate more ideas per minute if they slowed down a little bit.
Articulation	Articulation is the distinctiveness or clarity of the words you say. Sometimes articulation problems are caused by a debater trying to go too fast. Other times they are attributable to a mush-mouth. The easy solution to this problem, besides slowing down a bit, is opening your mouth wider and putting effort into finishing your words.
Pronunciation	Correct pronunciation—saying your words correctly—is important. Your credibility can be greatly undermined if you mispronounce words or confuse two words that sound alike. Don't overreach on your vocabulary. Listen to how other speakers say certain words. You can also use a dictionary to see how words are pronounced.

APPENDIX 23: ADVANCED SKILLS—NON-VERBAL

Non-Verbal Skills	Description
Appearance	The way you are dressed sends signals to those around you. If you are underdressed, some may think you aren't professional and don't take the activity seriously. If you have poor hygiene (messy hair, unshaven), it may convey the same lack of respect.
Gestures	Gestures can help to emphasize points but undermine your goal if they appear forced, stiff, are poorly timed, or seem unconnected to the message. As long as the gestures are natural, connected to their message, and not overused, they can be an effective way to emphasize what you are saying.
Body Language	The way you stand, walk, and move during your speech conveys information to your audience. If you seem hesitant when preparing to speak, it sets a bad tone. If you slouch, pace nervously, or sway, it sends a negative signal to the audience and can be distracting. Debaters should stand up straight. Walk up to the podium and back from the podium in an upright, confident way.
Eye Contact	Eye contact can be an important aspect of communication. Debaters should establish eye contact at the start and conclusion of their speech, as well as many times in between. This enables you to make a connection with your audience and receive feedback about if and how your argument is being received.
Facial Expressions	Some debaters think they need to be stone-faced to convey seriousness or take facial expressions to such an extreme that they appear phony. Debaters should convey a sense of friendliness and goodwill by smiling before they start to speak. Don't force your facial expressions.

APPENDIX 24: ASSESSING DEBATERS

Debate Section	Did student . . .	Score (/5)	Additional Comments
Introduction	Define the topic? Present team's position clearly? Outline briefly what the team will talk about?	☐	
Body	Reaffirm team's position? Provide evidence, arguments, examples that support team's position? Present logically connected, cited, and concise arguments?	☐	
Questions	Ask good questions clearly and based on cited evidence? Answer questions effectively based on previous arguments?	☐	
Conclusions	Restate position? Present a summary of case? Acknowledge and answer best counterargument? Conclude case for the team?	☐	

Delivery and Approach	Did Student . . .	Score (/5)	Additional Comments
Eye contact	Pan the room and not look at ceiling/floor? Make eye contact?		
Presence	Look natural, add emphasis, and stand straight? Not pace or sway?		
Voice and Presentation	Use appropriate volume, enunciate, pause when appropriate, and speak clearly?		

OVERALL		Score (/10)	
	Presented arguments in a competent, consistent, and compelling way?		

NOTES

1. J. Wheeldon, R. Chavez, R., and J. Cooke. 2012. *Diagrammatic Debate and Dialogue: Handbook for the Use of Debate in WA Correctional Settings* (Olympia, WA: CRCC Education Program Office, Department of Corrections).

2. See S. Klein, M. Tolbert, R. Bugarin, E. F. Cataldi, and G. Tauschek. 2004. "Correctional Education: Assessing the Status of Prison Programs and Information Needs." (Washington DC: Department of Education, Office of Safe and Drug-Free Schools). Available at: https://www.cedatanetwork.org/pdf/corred_report.pdf

3. D. Brazzell, A. Crayton, D. A. Mukamal, A. L. Solomon, and N. Lindahl. 2009. *From the Classroom to the Community: Exploring the Role of Education During Incarceration and Reentry* (Washington, DC: Urban Institute); see also E. Greenberg, E. Dunleavy, and M. Kutner. 2007. *Literacy Behind Bars: Results from the 2003 National Assessment of Adult Literacy Prison Survey* (Washington, DC: National Center for Education Statistics).

4. Reported in D. Brazzell, A. Crayton, D. A. Mukamal, L. Solomon, and N. Lindahl. 2009. *From the Classroom to the Community.*

5. See J. Wheeldon. 2011. "Visualizing the Future of Post Secondary Correctional Education: Designs, Data, and Deliverables," *The Journal of Correctional Education* 62 (2): 94–116.

6. See J. Vaske, K. Galyean, and F. T. Cullen. 2011. "Toward a Biosocial Theory of Offender Rehabilitation: Why Does Cognitive-Behavioral Therapy Work?" *Journal of Criminal Justice* 39, no. 1: 90–102.

7. D. A. Andrews, J. Bonta, and R. D. Hoge. 1990. "Classification for Effective Rehabilitation: Rediscovering Psychology," *Criminal Justice and Behavior* 17: 37.

8. For a detailed overview, see Wheeldon, "Visualizing the Future of Post Secondary Correctional Education."

9. See International Debate Education Association, http://idebate.org/about/debate/why

10. A great example of such calls for new approaches can be found in A. D. Louden, ed., 2010. *Navigating Opportunity: Policy Debate in the 21st Century* (New York: International Debate Education Association Press).

11. For more see: S. K. Hunt, D. Garad, D., and G. Simerly. 1997. "Reasoning and Risk: Debaters as an Academically At-Risk Population," *Contemporary Argumentation and Debate* 18: 48–56; J. E. Rogers. 2002. "Longitudinal Outcome Assessment for

Forensics: Does Participation in Intercollegiate Competitive Forensics Contribute to Measurable Differences in Positive Student Outcomes?" *Contemporary Argumentation and Debate* 23: 1–27; J. E. Rogers. 2005. "Graduate School, Professional, and Life Choices: An Outcome Assessment Confirmation Study Measuring Positive Student Outcomes Beyond Student Experiences for Participants in Competitive Intercollegiate Forensics," *Contemporary Argumentation and Debate* 26: 13–40.

12. For more examples and experience, see B. L. Jackson. 1990. "Debating *Huck Finn*," *College Teaching* 38: 63–66; M. W. Firmin, A. Vaughn, and A. Dye. 2007. "Using Debate to Maximize Learning Potential: A Case Study," *Journal of College Teaching & Learning* 4, no. 1: 19–32; M. Pernecky. 1997. "Debate for the Economics Class—and Others," *College Teaching* 45, no. 4:136–138.

13. A. Vats. 2010. "Civic Engagement Through Policy Debate: Possibilities for Transformation" in *Navigating Opportunity: Policy Debate in the 21st Century,* ed. A. D. Louden 242–249 (New York: International Debate Education Association Press).

14. See the useful overview in R. Akerman and I. Neale. 2011. "Debating the Evidence: An International Review of Current Situation and Perceptions" (Reading, Berkshire, UK: CfBT Education Trust). Available at: http://debate.uvm.edu/dcpdf/ESU-Summary_debatingtheevidence.pdf

15. Traditional styles include Parliamentary, Policy, Public Forum, and Lincoln-Douglas debates. See *Navigating Opportunity: Policy Debate in the 21st Century,* ed. A. D. Louden 242–249 (New York: International Debate Education Association Press).

16. Jay Caspian Kang.2012. "High School Debate at 350 WPM," *Wired Magazine,* January 20, 2012. Available at: http://www.wired.com/magazine/2012/01/ff_debateteam/

17. In general, see W. Keith. 2007. *Democracy as Discussion* (Lanham, MD: Lexington Books). Keith revisits some of these points in his 2011 keynote address, "A New Golden Age–Debate in the 21st Century." Text for this speech can be found in A. D. Louden, ed., *Navigating Opportunity: Policy Debate in the 21st Century* (New York: International Debate Education Association Press), 11–26.

18. For some examples, see J. Heinrichs. 2007. *Thank You for Arguing: What Aristotle, Lincoln, and Homer Simpson Can Teach Us About the Art of Persuasion* (New York: Three Rivers Press); see also, A. D. Louden, ed., *Navigating Opportunity.*

19. For example, in R. E. Edwards. 2008. *Competitive Debate: The Official Guide* (New York: Alpha Books). The author, an award-winning and internationally recognized debate coach, advises students to simply type search terms into online search engines to find points to support their position. Nowhere is the importance of assessing the quality of the information discussed; the importance of using academic or otherwise

credible sources to strengthen one's case is subordinated to rhetorical tricks to persuade different audiences.

20. See Ronald L. Akers. 1998. *Social Learning and Social Structure* (Boston: Northeastern University Press).

21. For more on the connections between learning and moral development, see J. Wheeldon. 2009. "Toward Common Ground: Restorative Justice and Its Theoretical Construction(s)," *Contemporary Justice Review* 12, no. 1: 91–100.

22. See B. Mezuk, I. Bondarenko, S. Smith, and E. Tucker. 2010. "The Influence of a Policy Debate Program on Achievement in a Large Urban Public School System" (paper presented at the annual meeting of the American Sociological Association, Atlanta, GA, August 14–17, 2010).

23. See the useful overview in R. Akerman and I. Neale. 2011. "Debating the Evidence."

24. Discussed in J. Jensen. 2008. "Developing Historical Empathy Through Debate: An Action Research Study," *Social Studies Research and Practice* 3, no. 1: 56–67.

25. Discussed in Ackerman and Neale, "Debating the Evidence: An International Review of Current Situation and Perceptions."

26. See S. Herbst. 2009. *Change Through Debate* (Inside Higher Education), http://www.insidehighered.com/views/2009/10/05/herbst

27. M. J. Umoquit, P. Tso, H. Burchett, and M. J. Dobrow. 2011. "A Multidisciplinary Systematic Review of the Use of Diagrams as a Means of Collecting Data from Research Subjects: Application, Benefits and Recommendations," *BMC Medical Research Methodology* 11, no. 11: 1–10.

28. See D. Poole and T. Davis. 2006. "Concept Mapping to Measure Outcomes in a Study Abroad Program," *Social Work Education* 25, no. 1: 61–77; R. H. Hall and A. O'Donnell. 1996. "Cognitive and Affective Outcomes of Learning from Knowledge Maps," *Contemporary Educational Psychology* 21: 94–101.

29. See, for example, Wheeldon and Ahlberg, *Visualizing Social Science Research*; J. Wheeldon. 2013. "To Guide or Provoke? Maps, Pedagogy, and the Value(s) of Teaching Criminal Justice Ethics," *The Journal of Criminal Justice Education* 24, no. 1: 97–121; J. Wheeldon. 2013. "Mapping Mixed Methods Research: Methods, Measures, and Meaning," *Journal of Mixed Methods Research* 4, no. 2: 87–102.

30. For more on mind maps, see T. Buzan. 1974. *Use of Your Head* (London: BBC Books). For more on mind maps in social science research, see Wheeldon and Ahlberg, *Visualizing Social Science Research*.

BIBLIOGRAPHY

Akerman, R., and I. Neale. 2011. "Debating the Evidence: An International Review of Current Situation and Perceptions." CfBT Education Trust: Reading, Berkshire, UK. Available at: (http://debate.uvm.edu/dcpdf/ESU-Summary_debatingthe evidence.pdf)

Akers, Ronald L. 1998. *Social Learning and Social Structure* Boston: Northeastern University Press.

Anderson, L., E. Northcutt, and J. Higgins. 2001. *GED Essay Book*. Boston: Steck-Vaughn Company/Houghton Mifflin Harcourt.

Andrews, D. A., J. Bonta, and R. D. Hoge 1990. "Classification for Effective Rehabilitation: Rediscovering Psychology." *Criminal Justice and Behavior* 17: 19–52.

Brazzell, D., A. Crayton, D. A. Mukamal, A. L. Solomon,, and N. Lindahl. 2009. *From the Classroom to the Community: Exploring the Role of Education During Incarceration and Reentry*. Washington, DC: Urban Institute.

Buzan, T. 1974. *Use of Your Head*. London: BBC Books.

Candela, L. 2003. "Ethical Debates: Enhancing Critical Thinking in Nursing Students." *Nurse Educator* 28: 37–39.

Combs, H. W., and S. G. Bourne. 1994. "The Renaissance of Educational Debate: Results of a Five-year Study of the Use of Debate in Business Education." *Journal on Excellence in College Teaching* 5: 57–67.

Edwards, R. E. 2008. *Competitive Debate: The Official Guide*. New York: Alpha Books.

Firmin, M. W., A. Vaughn, and A. Dye. 2007. "Using Debate to Maximize Learning Potential: A Case Study." *Journal of College Teaching & Learning* 4, no. 1: 19–32

Greenberg, E., E. Dunleavy, and M. Kutner. 2007. *Literacy Behind Bars: Results from the 2003 National Assessment of Adult Literacy Prison Survey*. Washington, DC: National Center for Education Statistics.

Hadizadeh, J. 2001. "An Interdisciplinary Course Centered on Student Debate of Current Environmental Issues." *Journal of Geoscience Education* 49: 44–49.

Hall, R. H., and A. O'Donnell. 1996. "Cognitive and Affective Outcomes of Learning from Knowledge Maps." *Contemporary Educational Psychology* 21: 94–101.

Heinrichs, J. 2007. *Thank You for Arguing: What Aristotle, Lincoln, and Homer Simpson Can Teach Us About the Art of Persuasion*. New York: Three Rivers Press.

Herbst, S. 2009. *Change Through Debate*. Inside Higher Education, http://www.insidehighered.com/views/2009/10/05/herbst

Hunt, S. K., D. Garad, and G. Simerly. 1997. "Reasoning and Risk: Debaters as an Academically At-Risk Population." *Contemporary Argumentation and Debate* 18: 48–56.

Huryn, J. S. 1986. "Debating as a Teaching Technique." *Teaching Sociology* 14: 266–269.

International Debate Education Association. "Why Debate?" http://idebate.org/about/debate/why

Jackson, B. L. 1990. "Debating Huck Finn." *College Teaching* 38: 63-66;

Jensen, J. 2008. "Developing Historical Empathy Through Debate: An Action Research Study. *Social Studies Research and Practice* 3, no. 1: 56–67,

Kang, J. C. 2012. "High School Debate at 350 WPM." *Wired Magazine,* January 20, 2012.

Keith, W. (2007). *Democracy as Discussion*. Lanham, MD: Lexington Books.

———. 2011. "Keynote Address: A New Golden Age–Debate in the 21st Century." 11–26. In *Navigating Opportunity: Policy Debate in the 21st Century,* edited by A. D. Louden. New York: IDEBATE, Press.

Klein, S., M. Tolbert, R. Bugarin, E. F. Cataldi, and G. Tauschek. 2004. "Correctional Education: Assessing the Status of Prison Programs and Information Needs. U.S. Department of Education, Office of Safe and Drug-Free Schools, https://www.cedatanetwork.org/pdf/corred_report.pdf

Kohlberg, L. 1981. *Essays on Moral Development*. Vol. 2, *The Psychology of Moral Development*. San Francisco: Harper & Row.

Logue, B. 1989. "A Captive Audience: Debating in a Maximum Security Prison." Presented at the annual meeting of the Speech Communication Association, San Francisco, November 18–21, 1989.

Louden, A. D., ed. 2010. *Navigating Opportunity: Policy Debate in the 21st Century*. New York: IDEBATE Press.

Mezuk, B., I. Bondarenko, S. Smith, and E. Tucker. 2010. "The Influence of a Policy Debate Program on Achievement in a Large Urban Public School System." Paper presented at the annual meeting of the American Sociological Association, Atlanta, GA, August 14–17, 2010.

Moeller, T. G. 1985. "Using Classroom Debates in Teaching Developmental Psychology." *Teaching of Psychology* 12: 207–209.

Osborne, A. 2005. "Debate and Student Development in the History Classroom." *New Directions for Teaching & Learning* 103: 39–50.

Pernecky, M. 1997. "Debate for the Economics Class—and Others." *College Teaching* 45, no. 4: 136–138.

Poole, D., and T. Davis. 2006. "Concept Mapping to Measure Outcomes in a Study Abroad Program. *Social Work Education* 25, no. 1: 61–77.

Proulx, G. 2004. "Integrating Scientific Method and Critical Thinking in Classroom Debates on Environmental Issues. *The American Biology Teacher* 66, no. 1: 26–33.

Rogers, J. E. 2002. "Longitudinal Outcome Assessment for Forensics: Does Participation in Intercollegiate Competitive Forensics Contribute to Measurable Differences in Positive Student Outcomes?" *Contemporary Argumentation and Debate* 23: 1–27.

———. 2005. Graduate School, Professional, and Life Choices: An Outcome Assessment Confirmation Study Measuring Positive Student Outcomes Beyond Student Experiences for Participants in Competitive Intercollegiate Forensics." *Contemporary Argumentation and Debate* 26: 13–40.

Umoquit, M. J., P. Tso, H. Burchett, and M. J. Dobrow. 2011. "A Multidisciplinary Systematic Review of the Use of Diagrams as a Means of Collecting Data from Research Subjects: Application, Benefits and Recommendations. *BMC Medical Research Methodology* 11, no.11: 1–10.

Vaske, J., K. Galyean, and F. T. Cullen. 2011. "Toward a Biosocial Theory of Offender Rehabilitation: Why Does Cognitive-Behavioral Therapy Work?" *Journal of Criminal Justice* 39, no. 1: 90–102.

Vats, A. 2010. "Civic Engagement Through Policy Debate: Possibilities for Transformation in *Navigating Opportunity: Policy Debate in the 21st Century*, edited by A. D. Louden, 242–249. New York: IDEBATE Press.

Wheeldon, J. 2009. "Toward Common Ground: Restorative Justice and Its Theoretical Construction(s)." *Contemporary Justice Review* 12, no. 1: 91–100.

———. 2010. "Mapping Mixed Methods Research: Methods, Measures, and Meaning." *Journal of Mixed Methods Research* 4, no. 2: 87–102.

———. 2011. "Visualizing the Future of Post Secondary Correctional Education: Designs, Data, and Deliverables." *The Journal of Correctional Education* 62, no. 2: 94–116.

———. 2013. "To Guide or Provoke? Maps, Pedagogy, and the Value(s) of Teaching Criminal Justice Ethics." *The Journal of Criminal Justice Education* 24, no. 1: 97–121.

———, and M. Ahlberg. 2012. *Visualizing Social Science Research: Maps, Methods, and Meaning*. Thousand Oaks, CA: Sage Publications.

———, R. Chavez, and J. Cooke. 2012. *Diagrammatic Debate and Dialogue: Handbook for the Use of Debate in WA Correctional Settings*. Olympia, WA: CRCC Education Program Office, Department of Corrections.

———, and J. Faubert. 2009. "Framing Experience: Concept Maps, Mind Maps, and Data Collection in Qualitative Research." *International Journal of Qualitative Methods* 8, no. 3: 68–83.

Notes

Notes

Notes

Notes

Notes

Notes